COLLECTOR'S GUIDE TO
AUTOGRAPHS

Wallace-Homestead Collector's Guide™ Series
Harry L. Rinker, Series Editor

Collector's Guide to Autographs, by Helen Sanders, George Sanders, Ralph Roberts
Collector's Guide to Baseball Cards, by Troy Kirk
Collector's Guide to Comic Books, by John Hegenberger
Collector's Guide to Early Photographs, by O. Henry Mace
Collector's Guide to Toy Trains, by Al and Susan Bagdade

COLLECTOR'S GUIDE TO
AUTOGRAPHS

GEORGE SANDERS, HELEN SANDERS, AND RALPH ROBERTS

Wallace-Homestead Collector's Guide™ Series

Wallace-Homestead Book Company
Radnor, Pennsylvania

Designed by Anthony Jacobson
Manufactured in the United States of America

Library of Congress Cataloging in Publication Data

Sanders, George R.
    Collector's guide to autographs / George Sanders, Helen Sanders,
Ralph Roberts.
        p.   cm.—(Wallace-Homestead collector's guide series)
    Includes bibliographical references and index.
    ISBN 0-87069-556-8
    1. Autographs—Collectors and collecting.   I. Sanders, Helen.
II. Roberts, Ralph.   III. Title.
Z41.S23   1990
929.8'8'075—dc20   89-51563
                                                         CIP

1 2 3 4 5 6 7 8 9 0   9 8 7 6 5 4 3 2 1 0

Contents

Foreword

Gaius Plinius Secundus, known as Pliny the Elder, was a great Roman scholar who perished while trying to observe closely the eruption of Mount Vesuvius in 79 A.D. He was also an autograph collector who prized in his collection a letter written by Julius Caesar. The great Caesar had died in Rome about 70 years before Pliny was born. Almost 2,000 years later, autographs are still being collected. Napoleon, Dickens, Gershwin, Lincoln, and Babe Ruth are just a few of the names that have gone down in history in their respective fields of endeavor and are currently being collected by those interested in autographs.

Looking at an engraving or photograph of a famous person is fine. Reading about that person in books can be interesting. But imagine actually holding a letter written by a famous personage of history. Abraham Lincoln, for example. You'd be holding a piece of paper that Abraham Lincoln actually held in his own huge hands! Abraham Lincoln! The guy on the penny. The one pictured on the five-dollar bill! You'd be holding genuine history in your hands. Abraham Lincoln once wrote that letter to someone, and you can have that letter in your personal possession. It was a part of Abraham Lincoln's important life. His thoughts went into that letter, into that piece of paper you can hold in your hand.

Or maybe you'll get to hold and own a requisition for food for hungry French troops, approved by Napoleon. Or a letter of Babe Ruth's, describing a monstrous home run. Or a note from Charles Dickens telling someone how much he enjoyed listening to "A Christmas Carol" being reread to him during the holiday season. Or a letter from George Gershwin explaining that he had decided to write a Broadway musical or a rhapsody concerning the color blue.

History, as you can see, comes alive with autographs. Instead of merely reading about someone's life, you can actually live it with him or her. The moments the famous person spent back in 1862 or 1798 or 1935, writing that letter or signing that document, are still alive. You are reading the words he or she wrote, years after they were written. It's a frozen moment in time, and you are the *guardian* of that moment. No one else on earth has it.

An autograph is not like a postage stamp, or a coin, or a baseball card. The piece of paper with an autograph on it is truly *one* of a kind. No one writes two letters to the same person on the same day with the same content. Each piece is a unique possession, and when you acquire such a possession you are entrusted with it—to preserve and protect it.

Pliny was the first recorded autograph collector at the beginning of the first millennium of modern history As you collect autographs you will be forming a collection of writings of the second millennium and carefully preserving those writings so that important pieces of history will survive into the third millennium. A monumental task, but you can do it!

How? Easy! *The Collector's Guide to Autographs,* by George Sanders, Helen Sanders, and Ralph Roberts, has been carefully written with you in mind. Whether you are a beginner or already a collector, you will find this excellent book of interest. In these pages the dynamic hobby of collecting autographs comes alive. Read this book carefully from cover to cover. When you are finished, keep it within reach, because as you are assembling your own valuable collection you will refer to it again and again.

Herman Darvick

Herman Darvick, founder and owner of Herman Darvick Autograph Auctions in New York City, the leading autograph auction firm in the United States, has been actively involved in autograph collecting since 1968, when he became president of the Universal Autograph Collectors Club, an office he held until he retired in 1987. He has been an autograph dealer since 1971, and he has taught a course on collecting autographs at Hofstra University in Hempstead, Long Island. The author of the popular children's book, *Collecting Autographs,* published by Messner Books/Simon & Schuster in 1981, Darvick is also a contributor to the *World Book Encyclopedia,* authoring the "Autograph" entry. He has been interviewed on the subject of autographs in hundreds of newspapers, such as *USA Today* and *The Wall Street Journal;* in magazines such as *Business Week* and *U.S. News & World Report;* and on radio and television by talk show hosts, including Oprah Winfrey and Joe Franklin.

Preface

To the enthusiastic seeker of autographs there can be no more genuine thrill than to receive a favorite personality's signature in person. As a professional broadcaster, interviewer, columnist, actor, master of ceremonies, radio and television news commentator, and ultimately, a longtime broadcasting executive in the United States and abroad, George Sanders had the good fortune of meeting the famous and infamous from every walk of life.

On motion picture sets, in radio and TV studios, in sports arenas, in public auditoriums, in their homes, in their offices and his, in over 100 foreign nations, and even in the White House, George had pen in hand so that the celebrity of the moment could accommodate the oft-spoken words, "May I have your autograph, please?"

In this book, we give you some samples of "photo opportunities" that clearly illustrate that most famous people are usually delighted to pose and oblige with their coveted autographs. These are some of the most cooperative signers we could find (with the exception of actor Paul Newman, as explained in the text), and we recommend that you search out these good folks.

Our sincere thanks are hereby extended to some of the world's greatest photographers, who opened their respective lenses to capture so many exciting moments in the Sanders' thrill-packed lives. These photo artists include Julius "Bud" Clauss, Charles D. Allegrina, Helen Doolittle Sanders, Al Boyer, Hal Jann, Carl Vermilya (KPTV-Channel 12 Portland, Oregon), Paul Snider, Bruce Luzader, Hollywood's Mac Julian (Warner Brothers), Academy Award–winning cinematographer William "Bill" Fraker (Paramount), Alex Jessen, O'Brien Photos, Photo-Art Commercial Studios, Earl Leaf (Republic, Eagle-Lion, Universal Studios), Lucretia and Floyd McCarty (Warner Brothers), Rod Tolmie (RKO Pictures), Rothschild Photos of Los Angeles, Ken Whitmore, Pat

Clark (Warner Brothers), and various staff photographers of MGM and 20th Century Fox, including J. Allen Hawkins, Irving L. Antler, Richard Wright Hutchinson.

Our grateful thanks go to Doctors Lewis C. Sommerville, Leslie A. Smart, Ronald R. Caldwell, and Wade Hampton Saunders for keeping us alive.

Special thanks go to our always helpful daughter, Susan Tracy Wadopian, whose constant love and encouragement made *retirement* a dirty word.

We must also express professional appreciation to our autographic colleagues Roger E. Gilchrist, Charles "Chuck" McKeen, Pat and Charles Searle, Jack "Charles" Ellison, and Sheila and Rhodes T. Rumsey for the expertise they so willingly shared.

Last, but in no way least, to those special little people we love, Joan Helen, Erin Elizabeth, Lael, Joel Sanders Wadopian, and Alexis Roholt, our grateful appreciation for remaining quiet and orderly while we toiled on this book. For grandchildren, aged ten years to fifteen months, that's really quite a lot.

George and Helen Sanders

Thanks go to my mother and to my sister, Marie Moseley, for their encouragement; to my brother-in-law Chuck and my nephew Taylor; to Angelika Burrus and to my god-daughter, Regan Joanna Burrus, on the occasion of her first book dedication.

Ralph Roberts

What Comes First?

Utterly ridiculous! Would you just look at that crowd of people! They have absolutely besieged that poor man. Why, he's completely surrounded. They seem to be handing him pieces of paper; then he scribbles something and gives the papers back. Everybody walks away quite contented and happy.

Surely you have seen just such a group at some kind of event or other—a major league baseball game, a movie premiere, a concert, a presidential campaign fund raising. You'll see it just about anywhere a celebrity might be found. Not always, but frequently this gathering is accompanied by pushing, shoving, and occasional screaming. Why? What makes ordinarily well-behaved human beings resort to such behavior?

It's the love of a hobby. It's the excitement of the hunt. It's the victory of the hunter and the trophy is something very, very special—an *autograph,* someone's *signature.* Not only is it personal, but it is also unique. It is orginal and one of a kind. There is not another one exactly like it in this whole, wide world. Collecting such autograph trophies is exceptionally interesting and lots of fun, and it can be tremendously profitable.

Why This Hobby?

No matter what your age or financial condition, if you are flirting with whether to *have* a hobby or deciding *which* one to get into let us assure you that *this* hobby, the collecting of autographs, can give you unmeasured enjoyment and unequaled thrills. This hobby can also give you a feeling of contentment that will overwhelm you as your collection grows and you are surrounded by things in which you can take pride.

You will not waste hours "experiencing" make-believe fun as a couch potato. You will not succumb to boredom if you happen to be snowed in for the winter. You will not

From left to right; prominent attorney Jack Crumley, former middleweight boxing champion *Barney Ross,* lightweight champion Lauro Salas, George Sanders, and Hollywood sports promoter Lenny Robbins.

Bobby Riggs   *Wm. T. Tilden*

Tennis immortals *Bobby Riggs* and *Bill Tilden* appeared with George Sanders during a tournament in Pasadena, California, in 1945.

be depressed when the heat of the summer or the spring rains keep you off the golf course. Instead, you will be ecstatically happy because those hours will be pleasantly filled as you act on your compelling desire to accumulate whatever you have chosen to collect out of the broad range of autograph specialties available.

No, you do not have to go on the prowl for your autographs or be part of a pushing, shoving crowd. Perhaps waiting at the stage door is not your thing—and there is a good

3

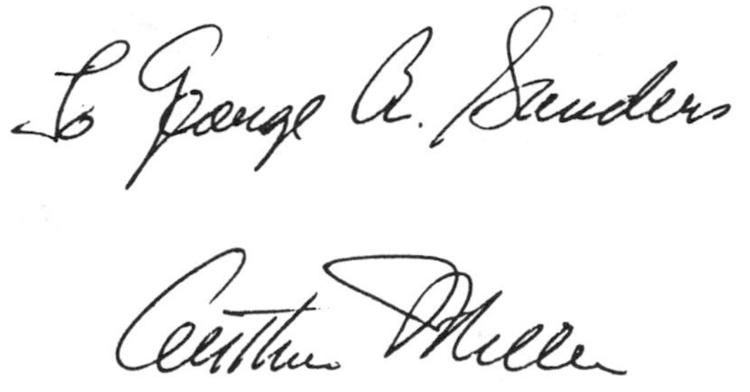

To George A. Sanders

Arthur Miller

Arthur Miller had recently divorced Marilyn Monroe when he signed George Sanders's guest book.

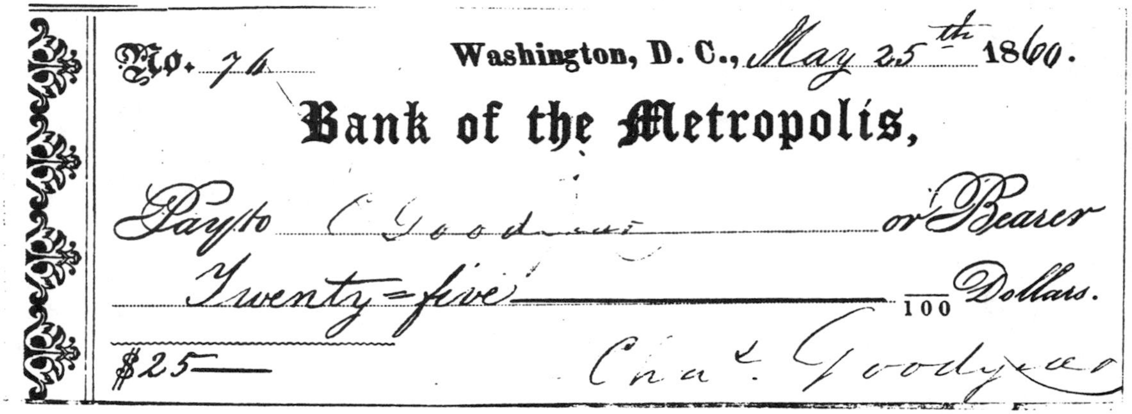

No. 76   Washington, D. C., *May 25th 1860.*

Bank of the Metropolis,

Pay to C Good____   or Bearer

Twenty-five   100 Dollars.

$25—   Chas Goodyear

Checks signed by inventor *Charles Goodyear* are selling for $2500 and will keep increasing in value.

chance that there is no major league team in your city. Besides that, you may have never laid eyes on a celebrity in your life, much less had one visit your town. However—you probably have a hero. There is probably someone you have always admired, maybe secretly, maybe openly. Tracking down an autograph from such a person might be a good place to start your autograph hobby because if your hero is a celebrity in any field there is something out there that he or she has signed.

Opportunities within the Hobby

So let us assume that you have decided to collect autographs. What is out there to collect? There's just about anything your heart desires. Male or female, historical or contemporary. Actors, actresses, artists, astronauts, authors, aviators, baseball players, composers, Civil War figures, and so on. These are only a few of the many collectible categories, and we are only up to *c* in the alphabet! The list goes on and on, and within each category you can specialize.

5

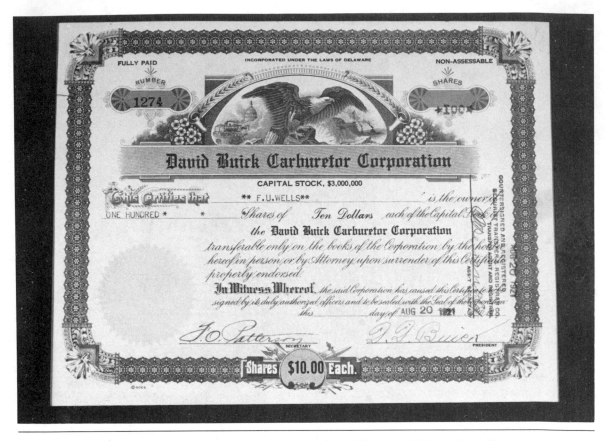

A stock certificate signed by *David D. Buick,* founder of the Buick Motor Car Company; rare in any form. Value: $600.

For example, if you have an interest in the Civil War then you may wish to pursue Confederate generals only. If your interest is baseball, members of the Hall of Fame may be the only figures you decide to represent in your autograph collection. You can collect in a single sport or in all sports, just as you can specialize in authors from the United States as opposed to British authors. You can focus on famous entrepreneurs or on political figures. And so on and so on.

Industrialist *Henry Ford* decided that this was his favorite photograph of himself, and he autographed a few for friends. Value: $2,000.

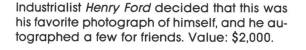

Willard J. Voit, founder and president of Voit Rubber Company tells George Sanders in 1952 how he became king of the sporting goods industry.

Sanders interviewed Attorney General *Robert Kennedy* for national television in 1961. Kennedy had just announced a huge crackdown on Mafia bosses.

The Magic of Autograph Collecting

Your choice of what to collect—what category and what specifics in that category—is almost unlimited, which gives you a versatility that very few other collectibles offer. Actually, stamp collecting is a collectibles field that gives you much the same options, but a stamp does not have the uniqueness of an autograph insomuch as there are millions of the same stamp issued, but the autographed card, photo, letter, or document you

Youthful Congressman *Ted Kennedy* shared a microphone with Sanders in 1959.

In October 1960, *Akihito,* then the crown prince of Japan, was introduced to Mrs. Hatfield by Oregon Governor Mark O. Hatfield. Portland Mayor Terry Shrunk and ABC news commentator Sanders attended the welcoming ceremonies for the prince and his princess, Michiko (barely visible at far left).

Sanders appeared on a 1960s television panel discussion program with Washington's Senator *Henry* "Scoop" *Jackson* (left).

Sincerely yours,

Margaret Chase Smith
United States Senator

Sanders chats with former U.S Senator *Margaret Chase Smith* of Maine during the Republican convention of 1964, held in San Francisco. Sanders was an ABC observer-commentator at several national political conventions.

Sanders fires a query at President *Lyndon B. Johnson* during a hectic election campaign.

acquire is an original. Such an autographed piece was signed only once, at a specific time and at a specific place, and was actually in the hands of the signer. That is the thrill of it.

One of the first things to learn about the fascinating field of autograph and manuscript collecting is that age alone means little. Why? Consider the flood of paper that you personally come in contact with weekly—grocery shopping lists, letters from Aunt Sally, canceled checks in your bank statement envelope, memos from the boss, your child's homework, recipes, casually scribbled reminders to yourself, and dozens more. A mountain of handwritten paper—signed and unsigned—towers in all our lives. And, folks, it has been this way for a very long time. Millions upon millions of documents have accompanied humankind down through the centuries. So a manuscript has to be extremely old to be worth much simply because of its age.

We may think that 1776 was long ago—really ancient times! But, as well-known autograph dealer Charles Hamilton states in his widely respected *Collecting Autographs and Manuscripts* (University of Oklahoma Press, 1974), the serious collector and dealer values European documents for their age only if they date from before 1400. According to Hamilton, in the United States the year that marks the dividing line between old and modern is 1650!

Why, then, do certain more recent autographs or manuscripts sell for thousands to a dealer or at auction? There are two reasons. The first is the more obvious—a piece will sell for a good amount if it includes a famous person's signature or has an association with that person in some manner. The second reason a piece will command a high value—historical or topical association—we will discuss shortly.

Excellent examples of value through association with a famous person are the letters of James Speed, Attorney General of the United States under Abraham Lincoln in 1864 and 1865. The Civil War and its aftermath overshadowed Speed, and he is now lost in the mists of history. But many of his official letters—written by his clerk and only signed by Speed—are now highly collectible. That clerk was Walt Whitman! Hence, the letters are valuable not for whose *autograph* is on them, but for the handwriting of the clerk who penned them. Knowing history and being able to prove association for a document can make a casual find, bought for a pittance, into a sought-after collectible worth hundreds or thousands of dollars.

Value

Autographs of celebrities are often cut out of letters and the signature sold alone, but an autograph is of greater value if it is still part of a letter or other manuscript. A note on White House stationery from Franklin D. Roosevelt is worth more, for example, than just his signed name, and one of Thomas Wolfe's novels autographed by Wolfe is worth

Any handwritten, signed letter from a U.S. president, such as this example by President *James A. Garfield,* brings a high price in the marketplace. Such a presidential document is worth even more if it was written while the person actually held the office of president. Value: $600.

Front and back of an executive card showing a brief letter written and signed by President *Grover Cleveland.* Value: $750.

Washington City,
August 20. 1845.

Dear Sir:

Your favor of 16th instant, covering a letter to Secretary Marcy, recommending Lieut. French for a post in the Quarter Master's Department, was duly received.

I have this morning transmitted your letter to the Secretary at War, accompanied by a note of my own, expressive of your strong claims to his favor, and of the high gratification a compliance with your wishes would afford me. Trusting that the application may prove successful,

I remain,
very truly,
Your friend,

James Buchanan

John M. Read, Esq.
Philadelphia.

Letter by President *James Buchanan*. Value: $1,200.

Secretary of the navy Dan A. Kimball and President *Harry S. Truman* at the White House. Sanders was on the guest list for this social gathering.

more than just the author's written name. Speaking of books, a caution is necessary here. It was common practice in the nineteenth century to include a facsimile of the author's signature in the front of books. These facsimiles are worthless. You can usually tell a genuine signing from a printed facsimile by holding the page up to the light and examining it from the back. If the ink has not penetrated into the paper, then it is probably a printed facsimile—which adds no value to the book.

The march of technology has continued to make the collection of celebrity autographs more difficult. Signing machines (the most common brand is the Autopen) have relieved busy politicians of the onerous duties of actually signing the many letters they send out. The name signed to an appeal for political donations from Gerald Ford, Jimmy Carter, or Ronald Reagan may look like a personal signature, but it isn't. Such mechanically reproduced signatures have no real value.

Going a bit further back, before mechanical signers, many of the notes from Dwight D. Eisenhower were signed for him by other people. Authentication of a person's signature by the collector requires comparison with a known signature by that person. Such firsthand authentication is often not possible, but buying autographs from a large, reputable dealer in autographs is one sure way of avoiding facsimiles or, worse, forgeries.

In today's fast-paced information age, computers are supplanting Autopens. For only a few hundred dollars, any celebrity with a personal computer can scan in his or her signature, construct a form letter, and, using a laser printer, send out thousands of authentic-looking signatures. Such signatures save celebrities time and money, but they add *no value* to your autograph collection.

Association and Diversification

The second value criterion for collecting manuscripts is historical or topical association. Just as a certain stamp collector might accumulate only stamps with the pictures of dogs or political figures, a document collector might specialize in presidential autographs or— as J. P. Morgan did when he began his famous collection— the signatures of Methodist and Episcopal bishops. A collector could gather letters of Civil War soldiers, or of doughboys in World War I, using a unified and interesting theme to make the whole worth more than its individual parts.

Although a person who holds autographs and manuscripts merely for their investment potential misses out on much of the magic enjoyed by the true collector, typically prices continue to increase for autographs so their value as an investment cannot be totally ignored. Hamilton's 1974 book gives the example of the refugees who left Nazi Germany

This signed photo of *Orville Wright* signing an autograph is quite a novelty. Once an inexpensive item, Wright's autographed pictures are currently selling in the $2,000 range.

at the onset of World War II. The lucky few who did manage to escape were stripped of all their jewels, family estates, paintings, and cash. They were passed by the border guards, in many cases, with only a handful of worthless old family papers. If Marshal Goering, an avid autograph collector, had realized the millions of marks that left the Third Reich as rare letters of Martin Luther, Voltaire, Beethoven, Napoleon, and others, he might personally have insisted on serving as a customs agent. Those fortunate people who got their assets out in this manner were able to sell them and start fresh in the New World—with some money in hand.

The advice that Hamilton and others give to someone who is starting an autograph collection is not to specialize too much, but rather to gather five or six different collections at the same time. Experts liken this to the way that a stock investor diversifies his or her portfolio. For example, if you had started collecting 30 years ago in the categories of science, music, World War I, Napoleon, and American Western autographs, your overall collection would have held its value, even though prices have declined in the World War I category. Actually, due to dramatic increases in music and science, the overall worth would be considerably more than your original outlay. Had you collected only World War I autographs, you would have nothing to balance their price decline and your collection would not have held its value.

Another important advantage of diversification is that you can afford to wait on "safe" buys, avoiding premium prices. If you are collecting a number of different categories, the opportunites for lower prices will be greater. Additionally, the wider selection of material will probably be more interesting—and researching into several fields will keep each field fresher and more exciting to you.

The Rewards

The true rewards of autograph and manuscript collection come not from financial gain but through the romance of holding true written history. The aura that seems to glow from a paper that George Washington touched and wrote upon, a check signed by Orville Wright, an autographed first edition of Mark Twain's, Napoleon's signature, or a letter from Theodore Roosevelt can warm you over the flame of our mutual heritage, as can, equally, the heart-touching letter of a Civil War soldier, little more than a boy, to his sister back home. All these and more are the attractions of owning and having these bits of history.

"Switching Horses"

Whatever you choose to be your specialty or specialties, you may find later on that your interests have changed or that you have grown out of a particular field and wish to switch horses in midstream. No problem. Just do it. If you have collected wisely your material should be readily salable or tradable at the autograph shows now held regularly all over the world and in every corner of the United States. Auctions are another source for selling, and, of course, other collectors and dealers are usually happy to purchase good material.

Starting Your Collection

Unlike other hobbies that require special hangers, holders, shelves, and space, collecting autographs involves collecting material that for the most part can be housed in standard-size binders to fit on standard-size shelves. Storage equipment is available at most office supply companies and at variety stores such as K-Mart and Woolworth's. Your very favorite items can always be framed and hung.

The start of your collection might well be hiding in an old shoe box on a closet shelf where mom and dad or, better still, grandma and grandpa tucked away some family treasure that they did not know was a treasure. There is always the chance of finding an old presidentially signed land grant or a canceled check endorsed or made out by a notable. Don't overlook those childish school days autograph books or your high school annuals. Maybe you remember that dad said he met Babe Ruth. "Sure!" you thought. But what a nice surprise if you found a baseball scorecard that the Bambino had signed.

Many collectors began what are today great collections by writing requests for signatures to contemporary celebrities. The targets are frequently seen on the covers of such magazines as *Time, People,* and *Sports Illustrated.* As previously mentioned, how-

A star-studded lineup of Hollywood personalities during a 1949 charity softball game. Back row, left to right: Sanders, 17-year-old actress *Elizabeth Taylor*, and *Shelley Winters;* front row, left to right: actors Marshall Thompson, Alex Cooper, and Carl Bailey, and the immortal *Nat King Cole.*

Stay Well —

Composer-singer *Roger Miller* with the entire Sanders family backstage during a 1967 concert. Back row, left to right: the concert's emcee George Sanders, son George Marston Sanders, and author Helen Doolittle Sanders; front row, left to right: son Stephen Gregg Sanders, Roger Miller, and daughter Susan Tracy Sanders.

ever, most material is acquired from dealers, auctions, and other private collectors. Collectors of any level can join the Manuscript Society and the Universal Autograph Collectors Club (U.A.C.C.) and subscribe to autograph collector's magazines and newsletters. To join the U.A.C.C. and the Manuscript Society, write to the addresses below:

U.A.C.C.
P. O. Box 467
Rockville Center, NY 11571

Manuscript Society
c/o David R. Smith
350 Niagara St.
Burbank, CA 91505

The nice thing about this hobby is that there is a tremendous source of material for your collection. The courteous, plentiful help and guidance you can receive from the aforementioned collectors and dealers will astound you.

There are no age barriers and no educational prerequisites. Whether you are a college graduate or grammar school student makes no difference. Nine or ninety, you can start

A signed first edition of *We Seven* features the signatures of all the original astronauts. Value: $750.

The lady with the lamp. Documents signed by the angel of Crimea, nurse *Florence Nightingale*, have always been collected. Because of its excellent content, this letter, which is half in ink and half in pencil because the writer ran out of ink while penning it, would sell for about $950.

your collection at any age. Regardless of age or education, you will be limited only by your ability to *ask* for an autograph, *write* for an autograph, or *purchase* an autograph.

Autograph collecting is truly a very special hobby. For example, if, on some occasion, you were able to purchase a Queen Elizabeth I document with her signature and beautiful *paraph* (a long, elaborate scroll under a signature) and, at another time, request and receive through the mail a simple signed photo of your favorite athlete, you now possess two inimitable items. One is far more valuable in dollar value than the other, of course, but you have acquired original pieces from two unrelated people, 500 years apart, and these pieces now have in common the fact that they reside in a single collection—*yours*. Once upon a time Queen Elizabeth I in the fifteenth century and your athlete in the twentieth century took a few seconds from their lives and put pen to paper. Those signatures are one-of-a-kind works of art. They also are historic moments in time. In this age of photocopies, photo reproductions, electronic form letters, and fax machines, can you see how extraordinary a genuine autograph becomes? Yes, very special!

So, what comes first? Well, as with everything in life, you have to make a decision. If you do decide that autograph collecting sounds like fun and that the constant search for material piques your interest and will continue to excite you, then you must make a commitment to yourself to search wisely and buy intelligently. Then, after some years go by and your collection grows, you will discover that you, too, have grown. You will find that the time and money you have spent was not wasted and that your investment in both has yielded a true treasure.

The History of Writing and Autographs

The history of autograph collecting is the history of writing. This chapter will give you an idea of the richness of the ages-old hobby of collecting signatures. We hope you will find it both entertaining and informative.

Our shaggy, cave-dwelling ancestors started the whole thing with drawings and paintings of animals on the walls of their cave condos many thousands of years ago. These drawings were not so much attempts to convey words as they were a means of pointedly suggesting to the totem spirits that hunting could stand to pick up. However, these drawings did get humans in the habit of taking notes—or making drawings—about what went on around them and what happened to them. Thus began the human habit of paperwork—make that *stone*work.

Prehistoric artists drawing bisons and mammoths on cave walls no doubt often personalized those drawings in some manner, thus inventing that unique and highly collectible entity, the *signature*. Alas, the collecting of caves is a time-consuming and bulky endeavor. The saving of *signed* documents did not start until five or six thousand years ago, when writing on more portable media came into being.

Heroes with Autographs of Clay

It was in the fertile crescent of the Tigris and Euphrates rivers—Mesopotamia, or modern-day Iraq—that bureaucracy (and, thus, writing) first got a leg up. For good or ill, the processing of the written word began there some 5,000 years ago with a people called the Sumerians, who preceded the Babylonians, the Hittites, the Assyrians, the Hebrews, and all the later civilizations who benefited so much from the innovations of the Sumerians.

The Sumerians invented concepts in mathematics, astronomy, astrology, business, and writing that still affect us today. The circle is divided into 360 degrees because of the Sumerians' use of 60 notation instead of our base 10, and complex geometrical problems—such as finding the areas enclosed in elaborate figures—were solved by Sumerian mathematicians. Sumerians watched the stars and named constellations and planets. They invented the signs of the Zodiac that those interested in astrology still use today, 4,000 years later. And it was the Sumerians who came up with a written language.

The Sumerians were smart, but they were resource-poor. They lived on the flat flood plains of the fertile crescent where there were very few stones or caves with walls to draw on. Nothing but millions and millions of tons of wet, gloppy clay mud.

Well we can imagine that some Sumerian, no doubt out looking for a cave or a stone, discovered *mud* as a substance to draw on. He may have tripped and fallen face-first into the gooey stuff, and, getting up, he may have noticed the impressions left by his clutching fingers. The art of word processing on clay tablets might have been born this way; most great discoveries happen by accident.

However they may have discovered mud as a medium of communication, the Sumerians developed a written language that was recorded on clay tablets. The writing started off, like most primitive writing, as mere pictographs. For example, a bird was drawn to represent the concept of *bird*. Easy to learn to write, if you had some artistic ability. The pictographs soon evolved into symbols, which probably saved the scribes a lot of time. A few specific wedge-shaped marks, pressed into wet clay with a reed stylus, came to indicate *bird*. Other symbols came into use for *fish* and *man* and *woman,* as well as for more abstract concepts, like "Greetings: Uncle Sum wants you."

This cuneiform (wedge-shaped) writing system was much too hard for the average Sumerian man-on-the-mud-flat to learn, so a class of professional word processors sprang up. These people went to school for long years to learn how to form all the different word symbols and how to select the best grade of mud to make clay tablets from.

For thousands of years in Sumeria and in the later city-states and empires that followed it, almost every transaction, no matter how small, was required to be recorded on a clay tablet and filed away. In Sumeria were born such common modern-day business practices of invoicing, inventory control, legal contracts, business letters, and bills. Not to mention duns for payment of said bills. Also, the Sumerians produced a rich body of literature, including stories such as the Saga of Gilgamesh, a flood story very similar to that of Noah in the Bible.

Hundreds of thousands of the Sumerian clay tablets have been found by archaeologists and many have been translated. Millions and millions of words were processed and recorded by means of this clumsy system, which worked well enough for 30 to 40 *centuries.*

The invention these ancient scribes came up with to keep contracts from being tampered with was pretty nifty. The scribes would write up a document on wet clay and have the two contracting parties impress their seal rings as signatures. Then the scribes would wrap an envelope of wet clay around the tablet and repeat the document on the outside of the envelope, again with the seal rings. In the event of a dispute (and the Sumerians had an elaborate court system) over whether the contract had been tampered with, the judge merely broke the outer envelope and checked to see if the inner document matched the outer. Everything—marriages, wills, loans, property transfers, sales of goods, diplomatic missions—was carefully regulated and recorded onto clay tablets in cuneiform writing.

And the clay tablet still has one amazing advantage over our present computerized word-processing, paper-oriented world. A clay tablet of cuneiform writing, even an un-baked one, is virtually everlasting. It won't mold away to dust in a few decades like paper. It won't rust or corrode like words inscribed on metal. And it won't eventually fade away like magnetic media. Clay is dirt and dirt doesn't rot. A clay tablet that has been in the ground since some Sumerian made it 3,500 years ago is probably still in good shape today and will be 3,500 years from *now*! (But just try to run one through a copying machine.)

"Signatures" were effected by pressing a seal ring onto the still-wet mud or by rolling a small cylinder onto the wet tablet which left a pictograph representing the person "signing" the tablet. Because of this method of signing, it is difficult to say that a particular pictograph is the autograph of a particular person, say, Hammurabi.

Hammurabi was a Babylonian king who lived about 1750 B.C. and ruled an ever-expanding empire for over 40 years. By the time he was born, writing on clay tablets had been in existence for thousands of years.

Hammurabi, because of the rich legacy of written history already in existence almost 2,000 years before the birth of Christ, was able to transport the recorded laws of the Sumerians and other predecessors to his own empire and codify them into a set of laws (called the Code of Hammurabi) which had a great impact on the course of human civilization.

To be able to examine a clay tablet setting forth these laws and say, "Yes, this seal is that of Hammurabi," would be fantastic. Any museum would pay millions of dollars for such an authenticated autograph. Unfortunately, literacy was the province of the professional scribes. They did the writing and probably pressed the signet rings into the clay. It is unlikely that mighty kings such as Hammurabi would soil their hands with *dirt*—but the thousands of years of writing tradition did set up the idea of *signing,* and the Egyptians followed through by devising a method of writing in which a person could actually make his or her personal mark. And of course the personal mark is the very basis of our wonderful hobby.

Write Like an Egyptian

Alas, for all their advantages, clay tablets did have a lot of drawbacks. They required a lot of special knowledge, were bulky to store, broke if you dropped them, and got your hands dirtier than heck with all that messing around in mud. So the ancient Egyptians took some time off from building pyramids to come up with something better. That something better was papyrus, the forerunner of paper and the source of paper's name.

Papyrus is a type of reed that grew in great quantity along the Nile river. The Egyptians developed a process of cutting the stalks of these reeds into thin strips and pressing them into sheets. These pressed sheets made excellent writing material, considerably easier to work with and store than clay tablets.

The invention of a paperlike substance gave word processing a terrific boost. Using pen (or brush) and ink gave tremendous flexibility over what could be depicted on this new writing material. The cuneiform writing of the Sumerians and Babylonians was limited to the types of characters that could be shown with wedge-shaped marks.

The Egyptian scribes who used papyrus found a much greater freedom in depicting their hieroglyphic writing system. Many of their papyrus manuscripts are still in existence, some dating to as far back as 4000 B.C.

To make books, the papyrus manuscript pages were pasted together in long rolls. One of the Egyptians' major religious books, *Book of the Dead* (copies of which exist in the British Museum today), is over 100 feet long when unrolled. And they produced many books in even greater lengths. (Some people have jokingly accused relatively modern wordy writers such as Charles Dickens of being paid by the word—maybe these ancients got paid by the roll or the cubit or whatever.)

The University of Michigan has a collection of over 7,000 papyrus manuscripts, and there are some 40 or 50 smaller collections in the United States alone. And, alas, hundreds of thousands of papyrus manuscripts decayed to dust and are lost forever.

The early Egyptian writing was hieroglyphic-based, meaning symbols were used for words. While specific symbols represented names, it is still hard to determine that one particular symbol is the actual autograph of King Tut, as opposed to being the handiwork of some scribe depicting the great king's name. Yet, by this time in history the tradition of signing was firmly established.

Partly as a result of the invasion of Alexander the Great, the Egyptian method of writing was drastically changed about 300 B.C. The Ptolemaic dynasty and later Roman occupation, for a few all-too-brief centuries, made Egypt the most literate in the world. The light that shone so brightly there was not to be duplicated again for almost 2,000 years!

It's All Greek to Some Collectors

The Greeks were responsible for inventing spelling. The ancient Egyptians' hieroglyphs, while elegant and artistic, were based on one symbol for a whole word, just as cuneiform marks had been. The Greeks came up with the first alphabet. (The word *alphabet* comes from the names of the first two Greek letters, alpha and beta.)

The alphabet added even more flexibility to writing. Now there was a method to indicate the sounds that made up words. Writing became much more compact and versatile.

The result of this type of writing is we can now start to pick out the handwriting, and thus the autographs, of individuals. There is an abundance of Egyptian documents from the third century B.C. (all in Greek), including original letters. The light of reason that shone during that period meant many more people were literate than had ever been so before in human history.

No doubt there were also many handwritten papyri in Italy and Greece, both signed and unsigned, in these times also. Unfortunately, few have survived except for a few charred remnants from such "time capsule" locations as the volcanic-buried cities of Pompeii and Herculaneum.

Many, many more Egyptian papyri would still exist if it had not been for the Arabs. In religious fervor, the Arabs destroyed thousands upon thousands of Egyptian manuscripts. The burning of the great library at Alexandria in A.D. 641 in a single act eradicated tens of thousands of documents covering many centuries and the largest collection of autographs to date. The light of reason burned only fitfully for hundreds of years after that despicable act.

The Romans

The Romans, in between conquering the known world and feeding critics to the lions (a practice some writers would like to see revived), continued to improve on the alphabet and the use of the written language. Most of our modern alphabet's letters come from the Greek and Roman alphabets. So more sophistication was added to writing, and literacy, though still restricted, became more widespread. No longer was it only scribes who could read and write; the newer system was much easier to learn.

Much of the literature of Greek and Roman times, and a lot of the everyday business transactions, has come down to us. Today copies still exist of Plato's dialogues, Julius Caesar's journey over the Rubicon, Cicero's *Republic,* and so on. We also have hundreds of thousands of words on more mundane matters such as the business correspondence of people like Irvus Goldsteinus, grain importer. Long, interminable bills of lading and the like. Makes you think, what are we leaving for our far-future descendants to pore over?

The Romans started the practice of requiring signatures on common legal documents such as deeds and contracts. The use of symbols or marks in place of a signature was relegated to the use of unlettered persons only. Thus, the use of autographs got a big boost.

Romans also gave the idea of *collecting* a big boost. In various writings Cicero and Pliny the Younger mention their manuscript collections, and other prominent Romans collected manuscripts as well.

Parchment, Vellum, and Paper

The Romans also added another writing medium to supplement papyrus manuscripts—parchment and vellum. Animal skins (mostly sheep) had the advantages of being easier to write on than papyrus, as well as being more plentiful throughout the empire. Except with a few animals who weren't really too thrilled about giving up their hides for the sake of literature or Irvus Goldsteinus's boring business correspondence, animal skins were a popular writing material down into the Middle Ages. (See section in Chapter 3 entitled "Parchment and Vellum" for more information on this topic.)

But! The wily Chinese had been just biding their time over on the other side of the ancient world. A fellow by the name of Ts'ai Lun, who was Emperor Ho Ti's minister of public works in A.D. 105, discovered *paper*! He had become dissatisfied with the bamboo and silk that were being used as writing materials in China at that time. Experimenting with the bark of the mulberry tree, he devised a method by which the fibers could be separated and pounded into a sheet. Later rags, hemp, and even old fish nets were used in the making of paper.

The art of papermaking spread. One way the art spread was via the capture of several Chinese papermakers by Arabs in about A.D. 795. A paper industry sprang up in Baghdad, and the Moslem world soon was enjoying the superiority of paper as a writing material. With the Moorish Arab conquest of Spain, the knowledge of papermaking spread to Europe, and word processing has not been the same since. It was like turning on the afterburner on a jet plane—things really took off.

An Illuminating Experience

Not that the acceleration was all that fast at first. If anything, during the early medieval period (the so-called dark ages) it slowed down a bit. Fewer people were literate. The literature of past glories was kept alive by monks in cold stone monasteries. The peasants were too busy being peasants, and members of the noble class were much too busy making jolly well sure the peasants *stayed* peasants. Nobody but the monks had much time to read. Or write.

However, in pure time-consuming effort, the diligent monks more than compensated for all the word processing *not* being done by the medieval populace in general. They turned manuscripts into pure works of art. Their manuscripts sported elaborate lines of red and blue, geometric figures, and green vine tendrils sprouting in the margins and twining gracefully around letters. The heavy use of color and decoration makes the surviving examples of such illuminated manuscripts almost priceless works of art today.

This monkish form of word processing certainly wasn't fast. The chief monk in charge of word processing had no chance of getting his section to churn out a report on the grape harvest by next Tuesday. Copy for the Abbot, copy for the Bishop, copy for the file? No way. So word processing was reserved for more important projects, like religious treatises or the copying of Aristotle's wisdom, and everyday paperwork was allowed to slide. A step backward from the days of Rome and Sumeria and Babylon, when practically every transaction was documented.

Thus, it is no accident that Xerox used monks in its television advertising a few years ago for both photocopiers and the Xerox 820 personal computer. Those poor but dedicated clerics, squinting with bleary eyes in dim candlelight, shivering in those drafty and cold monasteries, kept word processing alive through the dark ages. (Too bad they aren't still around to get royalties from Xerox's advertising, or a stock option at the very least.)

A few people who weren't monks learned to write also. The earliest known autograph of a lay person (i.e., not a monk or other cleric) is that of El Cid, the famous Spanish leader. This signature dates from 1096! King Richard II of England (1367–1400) is one of the earliest English kings whose writing is preserved. At least three known autographs exist. His successor, Henry IV, was a more ready writer, and several examples of his signature are in the British Museum and the Record Office. By that time, writing was becoming, for the first time since the Romans, a widespread accomplishment. So all this mostly monkly scribbling during the dark ages was but the lull before the storm.

The Printing Press

The Sumerians first used a written language on a large scale, the Egyptians came up with papyrus and made word processing more flexible, the Greeks and Romans provided a quantum leap by developing an alphabet, and the Chinese developed paper—but the Germans topped everybody by inventing the printing press.

The problem with word processing for wide dissemination up to this time had been that everything had to be copied by hand. There wasn't a Book-of-the-Month Club—or even a Book-of-the-Year Club. Nobody could write that fast. So books existed in a very, very few lavishly embellished copies and were the province of the privileged. A bestseller might be three hand-tooled leather-bound volumes encrusted with precious and semi-precious stones. At least there were no problems with remainders gathering dust on bookstore shelves! Not until Johann Gutenberg invented the movable type printing press in 1440.

Gutenberg came up with the great idea of making a metal casting of individual letters (in mirror image so that they would come out right on the paper). He could then combine these letters into words to make up the whole page of a book. Then, affixing his page plates in a press (he probably got this inspiration from seeing the wine and cheese presses of the time), he could ink a plate and press paper against it to get an image, as many times as he *wanted* to. Printing was nifty. And neat. And relatively inexpensive.

The development of the printing press was *important*. Books could suddenly be turned out by the hundreds of copies on Gutenberg's marvelous press. And, leaving off the gemstones, they could be produced rather cheaply. Books were now within the means of the average person, not just those in the noble classes. The percentage of literate persons began to increase at an ever-growing rate. More people being able to read and write meant there were more autographs to collect—and more people interested in collecting them.

By 1500 the use of printing was firmly established in Europe. Juan Pablos started the first print shop in the New World in Mexico City in 1539. The first print shop in what was to become the United States was opened by Stephen Daye at Cambridge, Massachusetts, in 1639. The new word-processing technology was proliferating rapidly, and it had become a part of everyday life.

As more people learned how to read and write, a lot more words began to go down on paper. Merchants again began to record their transactions. More people were writing books. Someone decided to publish Shakespeare's plays. The legal profession started recording many more accounts of the affairs of humankind than ever before. Contracts became more verbose. Poetry was written. Business letters proliferated in white blizzards. Word processing was definitely picking up by the beginnings of the Industrial Age in the late 1700s and early 1800s.

The role of the scribe of ancient times and the monks of the dark ages was now assumed by the secretary and bookkeeper in business, government, and academic circles. Usually these were pale men (epitomized by Dickens's Bob Cratchit in *A Christmas Carol*) who sat on high stools, hunched over a ledger book or sheets of correspondence. Their fingers were ink-stained. Bowls of sand to blot ink and dabs of sealing wax lay handy at their aching elbows. Writer's cramp was their constant companion. Words flew thick as snow in a Greenland winter.

A good many of the documents produced required signatures, thanks to the influence of the Romans. The idea of people, both famous and not, signing their names to letters, contracts, and deeds became firmly entrenched as a part of everyday life. Autograph collecting, as a result, began to take off.

Early Collectors of Note

In the sixteenth century, collectors came up with the concept of carrying around a book with blank pages for noted personages to sign. One of these autograph albums, dating from 1578, is preserved in the British Museum. Autograph albums notwithstanding, the signatures of some notables of that time are scarce. Of William Shakespeare's signature, for example, there are only six authentic examples known.

According to an article by Joseph E. Fields in *Autographs and Manuscripts: A Collector's Manual* (Scribner's, 1978), there were a number of important collectors in the sixteenth century. Antonine Lomenie de Brienne, a Frenchman, had a collection of 340 folio volumes, which are now preserved in the Bibliotheque Nationale. Philippe de Bethune (1560–1641) and Roger de Gaignieres (born in 1641) also spent their days and fortunes collecting letters and manuscripts.

Nor was France the only haven for collectors. The Germans Thomas Rehdiger (1540–1576) and Ludwig Camerorius (1573–1651) amassed considerable collections, as did Sir Robert Bruce Cotton (1556–1631) in England. A number of other prominent English collectors of this time left significant legacies. Their collections formed the basis for the British Library, the British Museum, and other priceless library collections. The collector, as is ever his or her privilege and mission, *preserves history*.

The eighteenth century is marked by collectors who were mostly wealthy nobles with the time and money to spend on collecting. The spread of literacy continued, and as the nineteenth century dawned, more and more people were able to engage in our delightful hobby.

Nineteenth-Century Collectors

To those who might doubt the information presented above and who might still believe that autograph collecting is a recent invention, we offer below an article from the *American Cyclopedia* (D. Appleton and Company, 1858). Edited by those nineteenth-century men of letters, George Ripley and Charles Dana, the following article on autographs shows how widespread the hobby was over 100 years ago.

A numerous and generally very intelligent body, scattered all over the civilized portions of the world, bear the name, from what they apply themselves to, of autograph collectors. . . .

It may be stated that those who ride the hobby of collecting autographs generally do it with higher purpose than mere curiosity. Whatever the original inducement, whenever the pursuit ripens into a passion, augmented knowledge, historical as well as biographic, is the result. A genuine collector is not satisfied with an autograph until he obtains as much information as possible concerning the writers. Very frequently the letter or document itself contains something which illustrates a doubtful point of history, or throws light upon an obscure passage of biography.

The largest private collection of modern times (i.e., the 1850s), in England, was that formed by the late William Upcott, of London. Upon his death it was sold by auction and dispersed. Sir Richard Phillips was a great collector, and claimed to be the first of the tribe.

"It is certain," says Catharine Hutton, "That he was in possession of these precious relics, each arranged by the alphabetical name of the writer. He was so well aware of their value, at a time when they were little thought of by others, that he has been heard to say he would as soon part with a tooth as a letter of Coley Cibber's; and that he expected a grant of land in America for a manuscript of Washington's."

There is another good collection in London, the property of Mr. Donnedieu, a Frenchman. Mr. Robert Dole, also of London, has a splendid collection—probably the largest in England, though he may be challenged by Mr. Dawson Turner of Great Yarmouth (surviving brother of the late Sharon Turner, the Anglo-Saxon historian), and the Rev. Dr. Raffles of Liverpool. These gentlemen have collections, each worth many thousands of pounds, and the arrangement of their treasures is at once simple and complete.

In Scotland, where autograph collectors are numerous, an Edinburgh bookseller, Mr. W. F. Watson, is confessedly the most successful and enterprising. Though a great portion of his treasures were obtained by exchange and gift, he has expended £15,000 on the purchase of rare autographs and costly portraits, views, maps, and title-pages to illustrate them.

In the United States, perhaps the most extensive collection has been formed by the Rev. Dr. William B. Sprague of Albany. In 1828, he commenced his collection, and much about the same time, Mr. Gilmor, of Baltimore, entered upon the same field. Mr. Gilmor's collection, which was very fine, has been much increased by Mr. Dreer, of Philadelphia, who purchased it.

Other eminent autograph collectors are Mr. Tefft of Savannah, Mr. Cist of Cincinnati (believed to reside now in St. Louis), Mr. Keeler of Mississippi, Mrs. Zachariah Allen of Providence, Mrs. T. A. Green and Miss Arnold of New Bedford, the Rev. Mr. Waterman of Boston, and Dr. Shelton Mackenzie (chiefly of modern European celebrities) now of Philadelphia. Mr. Charles B. Norton of New York has probably the largest public collection of autographed letters in this country.

For the information of collectors, who abound in the United States, we may mention that Dr. Sprague's mode of arrangement is twofold—one alphabetical, the other according to subjects, and one being to a great extent a duplicate of the other. He possesses (what is extremely rare) complete sets of the signers of the American Declaration of Independence, framers of the Constitution, generals of the revolution and, with a very few exceptions, of the members of the old congress.

Autograph collectors ought to be held in esteem, as often saving from oblivion or destruction many documents of great value. The original of the Magna Carta, now in London, was actually in a tailor's hands, for the purpose of being cut up into parchment measures, when it was rescued by an antiquary who fortunately knew its value and preserved it as an object of national interest and importance.

Into the Twentieth Century

Two collectors of note during the late nineteenth and early twentieth centuries were J. P. Morgan and Henry E. Huntington. Both men formed large and important collections now housed in the libraries named after them (the Morgan Library is in New York and the Huntington Library is in San Marino, California). Newspaper tycoon William Randolph Hearst was also a significant collector during this period.

No history of autograph collecting would be complete without a mention of that premiere autograph dealership, Walter R. Benjamin Autographs. Founded by Walter R. Benjamin and his brother William in 1887, the business continues to be preeminent in the field today, even though it is over 100 years old! Even more astounding, during this period, it has only had two managers—Walter R. Benjamin and his daughter, Mary A. Benjamin.

There are other collectors and dealers of note in the twentieth century, in fact, many, many more. To do the history of autograph collecting true justice would require an entire book by itself. For now, however, let us move on to the practicalities of collecting autographs.

The Basics

Probably the longest word you will have occasion to use in describing autograph collecting is *philography*. It is a word coined many years ago by authority Charles Hamilton. So just as a stamp collector is a *philatelist* and a coin collector is a *numismatist,* you will be (or already are) a *philographer*.

The Language of Autographs

Since autograph collecting is primarily a mail-order business, it is important to understand the abbreviations that are commonly used. If you know your ABC's you will have no difficulty in learning or understanding these basic abbreviations. You will need to know them because all dealer and auction catalogs use the abbreviated descriptions to tell potential buyers what an item is. There are some variations in these alphabet shortcuts, but a little common sense will see you through.

Before we take a look at the terminology abbreviations, however, let us try to clarify the meaning of two words, *autograph* and *holograph*. They are often used interchangeably, yet there is a subtle difference.

The word *autograph* is derived from the Greek *auto* (''self'') + *grapho* (''to write''). Its common usage outside the hobby denotes a person's signature, written by his or her own hand. However, the accepted usage by autograph collectors means *anything* that is written in a person's own hand, including an unsigned letter, a musical notation, an entire document, an artist's sketch, a page of written script, or an independent signature.

The word *holograph,* also from the Greek, comes from *holos* (''whole'') + *grapho* (''to write''). At one time this was the common English term for a letter or document written in the signer's own hand. It is still used to describe some letter or document items, but the most widely recognized word for this type of collectible here in the United States is *autograph*.

So that there will be no confusion in the text that follows, in a description of a letter, note, document, manuscript, or quotation, the word *autograph* means that the item is completely handwritten by the signer. When the word *signed* is used, it means that the item is actually signed—not printed, not stamped, not produced by Autopen.

The abbreviations in the following list may appear with or without periods.

A.L.S.: Autograph Letter Signed. A letter completely in the hand of the person described and signed by the same person.

A.L.S. or A.L. in third person: Autograph Letter Signed that contains the signature in the body of the letter; for example, "Mr. Charles Dickens thanks you for your comments. . . ."

A.N.S.: Autograph Note Signed. Same as A.L.S. except it is a note rather than a letter. A note commonly has no salutation or ending; however, an A.N.S. is frequently substituted mistakenly for an A.L.S.

L.S.: Letter Signed. The body of the letter is written by someone other than the person described as signer.

C.S.: Card Signed. It would be more common today to find just a SIG (see next entry).

SIG.: The described person's signature. Such a signature is frequently found on a 3 × 5 card or has been cut from a letter or document. Sometimes it can be signed with an inscription, date, place, or title (one or all of these). The signature might stand alone or with a group of others.

T.L.S.: Typed Letter Signed. This description is used by many collectors to further describe an item. The letter or note (*T.N.S.*) may or may not have been typed by the person described, but it is always signed.

T.N.S.: Typed Note Signed.

D.S.: Document Signed. Any sort of official government paper, bank check, military commission, appointment, pardon, or receipt that has been signed, docketed, or endorsed by the described person with the body of the document printed, written, or typed by another person.

A.D.S.: Autograph Document Signed. Same as D.S. only the body of the document is also written by the person described as signer.

Q.S.: Quotation Signed. A quotation (of the signer or another person) that is signed. The quotation may be typed, printed, or written in another hand.

A.Q.S.: Autograph Quotation Signed. Same as Q.S. only quotation is written by signer.

MusQS: Musical Quotation Signed. A few bars of music of a composer or music made famous by that person, with or without lyrics, signed.

AMusQS: Autograph Musical Quotation Signed. Same as MusQS with the bars of music written by the signer.

MsS.: Manuscript Signed. Usually a short story, play, poem, or anything else that has been prepared for publication or portion thereof and signed.

AMsS.: Autograph Manuscript Signed. Same as MsS only manuscript is in the hand of the signer.

TsS.: Typescript Signed. A further embellishment of MsS; a typescript is a page (more or less) of the described person's work, typed by someone other than the described person and then sent to him or her to be signed.

S.P.: Signed Photograph.

S.P.I. or I.S.P.: Signed Photograph Inscribed to a specific person.

P.C.: Post card.

The book printing industry prior to the nineteenth century is largely responsible for descriptions of size that are standard in the antiquarian book trade. Standard sheets of paper measuring 19″ × 25″ were usually printed and then the sheets were cut into pages. From this 19″ × 25″ paper, the following were derived:

Folio: Cut two from a standard sheet; each resulting sheet measures about 12″ × 18″.

4to, quarto: Cut four from a sheet; each resulting sheet measures about 9″ × 12″.

8vo, octavo: Cut eight from a standard sheet; each resulting sheet measures about 6″ × 8″.

12mo, duodecimo: Cut twelve from a standard sheet; each resulting sheet measures about 4″ × 6″.

16mo, sixteenmo: Cut sixteen from a standard sheet; each resulting sheet measures about 3″ × 5″.

Interpreting Catalogs

The sizes listed above have become an approximation in many of today's catalog descriptions. In some cases the item is smaller than is described, so if size is important to you it is well to ask for the exact dimensions of whatever you are ordering. For instance, an SP described as 4to is usually a standard 8″ × 10″ photograph but has become through usage accepted as 4to. The same applies when ordering an 8vo photograph, which is accepted as being approximately 5″ × 7″, and a 16mo piece, which is frequently smaller than 3″ × 5″.

These size approximations have come about through the cataloger's eagerness to save time and keystrokes when typing up a list. Rather than getting out a ruler to measure accurately the dimensions of the hundreds of pieces that make up a catalog, the cataloger makes an educated guess. So when you read a description be aware that the stated size may well be an estimate of a piece's relative size rather than a statement of its true dimensions.

Catalogers may be somewhat careless in distinguishing differences that arise in other categories of description. For example, a letter has a salutation: Dear Mom, Dear Mr. X, or just Hey, You! Something described as an N. Note does not have a salutation but may have a closing. A note, because it could be quite lengthy, might sometimes be described and sold as an L.S. or A.L.S. This could be an oversight and make no difference to you, but just the same, be aware that there is a difference which may not be revealed in the cataloger's descriptions.

In most cases, however, catalogers are quite accurate in their descriptions and even make an effort to list faults. Obviously, the catalogers do this so that you, the reader, can order from a catalog and expect to receive in return the item as described. Some catalogs are very detailed, while others are very sketchy. The presence of a long description of a piece does not necessarily mean that the piece is better than an item presented via a shorter description. In fact, one highly respected autograph dealer, who has since passed away, had the knack of writing "one-liners" that always seemed to impart to the reader everything he or she needed to know about the item for sale.

It is only fair to say at this time that in purchasing autograph material for a period of approximately 50 years from hundreds of different dealers both here and abroad, we have *never, never* been cheated. We may have returned pieces for one reason or another, but in these cases the purchase price was always returned or credit given. This industry has thus far maintained a very high ethical standard.

A catalog or advertised item might read as follows:

EDISON, THOMAS A. (Inventor) 1847–1931. A.L.S., 1p, 8vo. Dec. 21, 1892. "Send seven cartons tungsten wire, etc." On Edison Botanical letterhead. Full signature. "N" in Edison slightly smeared; otherwise dark and clear. $675.00

This description tells you who wrote the letter, what he was, and when he was born; specifics about the letter itself tell you date written, number of pages, size of page, indication of content, faults, and price. If the letter had an exceptionally interesting content, other parts or all of it might be quoted.

You will sometimes see the expression "integral address leaf attached." Before the envelope came into common use, sometime around the Civil War, a large sheet of paper about 12″ × 18″ was folded in half to form a four-page booklet with each page measuring 9″ × 12″. The letter was written on pages one through three, and the fourth page was left blank. The booklet was folded by turning the two blank outside edges of the 12″ side toward the center creating a piece folded in thirds. One side (third) was then tucked into the other side. This sounds a bit confusing, but give it a try. The result is a neat self-mailer—an *integral address leaf*—which is secured by sealing wax and addressed on the opposite blank side.

Frank Words about Franking

If the author of a letter is a member of Congress, he has a *franking* privilege, which means he does not have to pay for his postage. In the past, the member merely wrote "Free" in the upper right-hand corner and signed his name above it. These *free franks* (FF) are very desirable to collect. Because the privilege was also extended to the president of the United States, the First Lady, the vice president, cabinet members, and personnel of the Armed Forces, always be on the alert for one of these highly collectible signatures that might slip by unnoticed.

While the franking privilege is still very much in effect, in the twentieth century members of Congress employ the printed frank. These reproduced facsimile signatures are virtually worthless.

The First-Day Cover

Another growth area in the autograph field is the *first-day cover* (FDC). For those of you who have collected stamps in the past the FDC is nothing new. Since this philatelic category has been carried over into the philographic genre, a few definitions are in order:

This very rare first-day cover signed by *Bobby Jones* features a postmark and cachet issued on the day in 1933 that the Augusta National Golf Club opened its doors. Value: $600.

FDC: First-Day Cover. The stamp used on the first day of its issue and retained on its envelope (cover) as evidence of first day posting.

FFC: First-Flight Cover. Same as FDC only stamp and envelope have been flown on first day of issue.

The FDC sports a commemorative or special postmark in conjunction with a printed (or sometimes hand-drawn) cachet tying it in with the new stamp. As such they are philatelic covers, but these FDCs are frequently sent off to be signed by a person or persons who may have a common bond with the subject matter of the new stamp and its cachet. As an example, the numerous space issues have been signed by many of our leading astronauts.

Since foreign countries regularly issue stamps honoring *living* American and foreign notables, these FDCs can oftentimes be signed by the person whose image is on the stamp.

Blocks of four stamps, particularly if the wide margin is intact, can be autographed, or a single stamp can be mounted on a 3 × 5 card with the autograph beneath it. Pablo

Picasso and Marc Chagall both designed stamps which they have signed below the attractively mounted stamp.

The abbreviations that have been presented so far (remember that they may appear with or without periods) are most of those commonly used to delineate the autograph material found in the average dealer or auction catalog. There are still others that could be added, but generally your common sense will help you figure out their meanings. Here are just a few more:

n.d.: No date, meaning the date was not indicated.

n.p.: No place from which letter was written is indicated.

n.y.: No year, meaning the year was not indicated.

The Paraph and Other Wondrous Things

There are numerous words in everyday usage that are particularly apropos to the descriptions we apply to autographs. *Paraph,* which was used earlier in this book, is a flourish made by the writer after his signature. Certainly one of the best known paraphs is that of Charles Dickens, which he added below his name. Thomas A. Edison, on the other hand, drew his paraph above his name, and it is referred to as his famous "umbrella" paraph. A few other everyday words are defined below, as they apply to autograph collecting:

Contemporary copy: Contemporary copy is a term that is often misunderstood. It refers to a copy of the original that was made at the time the original was written or shortly thereafter. The word *contemporary* refers to the fact that the copy was made at a time contemporary with the initial piece.

Docket: A docket is a filing notation made on the back (verso) of a document or letter. The docket might contain the name of the writer, a date, and perhaps the subject of the letter or document.

Endorsement: An endorsement is normally thought of as the signature on the back of a check, but there is a further meaning for the term in the parlance of our current topic. In autograph collecting, an *endorsement* is also a notation on the verso of a letter or document, but it can be a permission, a denial of permission, or sometimes an acceptance. Civil War documents and letters provide a vast fund of *endorsements* with as many as three or four on a single piece.

M.C.: M.C. denotes a member of the Congress of the United States. The designation is used for all senators and representatives after the U.S. Constitution was adopted in 1787.

M.O.C.: M.O.C. refers to a member of the Old Congress (Continental Congress), which was in session from 1774 to 1789.

Modern: In autograph collecting, so-called modern autograph material dates from the sixteenth century forward.

Oblong: The term *oblong* (*obl*) can refer to any long narrow sheet of no specified size. Catalogs may further define a narrow sheet as *oblong quarto* (obl. 4to) or *oblong folio* (*obl. fol.*).

Old: The term *old* (as opposed to *modern*) for autograph material refers to pieces from the fifteenth century or earlier. United States autograph material that predates 1650 is considered old.

Provenance: The validity of an autograph item may be extremely important. Tracing its heritage is akin to acquiring a title insurance policy on a piece of property you purchase. Since there are no such legal instruments available for autograph material, you can ask for some kind of provenance—or history—for an item. That history may or may not be available for a particular item, but it certainly does not hurt to ask.

SIGNER: Spelled with all capital letters, the term *SIGNER* is used to identify any of the men who signed the Declaration of Independence, as well as those who signed the Constitution (for whom the phrase "of the Constitution: is added to SIGNER). A further designation, *signed,* in lowercase, indicates a signer of any other document on which there might be multiple signatures (such as treaties, charters etc.).

It is highly probable that your specialty will not be ancient or medieval manuscripts, but occasionally you will find letters and documents of a more recent era written on parchment or vellum. These two words are often used interchangeably, but they do not describe the exact same thing. *Parchment* is the treated skin of a sheep or goat which has been prepared for writing. *Vellum* is calfskin, lambskin, or kidskin, which has a superior writing surface after its preparation because it is finer and thinner. They are both used today, although infrequently, for some official documents.

If you have a question regarding the authenticity of a manuscript dating from the Renaissance on, then you should have at least some knowledge of paper. It is helpful to know that before the middle of the nineteenth century paper was made from rags and can be one of two types, *laid* or *wove*. When *laid* paper is held up to the light the marks of the metal wires stretched across the wooden frame mold used in its manufacture are visible. They are about 1″ apart and are known as *chain lines. Watermarks,* those translucent designs produced by thin wire patterns in the paper mold, can sometimes be of help in identifying and dating a piece of autograph material.

Most paper made before the middle of the eighteenth century shows chain lines. Because *wove* paper was considerably cheaper to produce than laid paper, it became more popular and began to be used in the second half of the century. Wove paper does not show any chain lines. Still less expensive to produce than either of these two rag-based papers was the paper that began to be manufactured after about 1860 with wood pulp as its base. This use of wood pulp ushered in an era of inexpensive but far more perishable paper. However, manufacturers continue to produce laid and woven rag papers, even into the late twentieth century.

Some illustrative terms now used in autograph collecting owe their origins to the book collectors, dealers, and catalogers who try to give as accurate descriptions as possible of the appearance of the manuscripts and other pieces they offer for sale. Some of these descriptive terms are listed below:

Browned (browning): Age gives a slight brownish cast to paper. Browning is practically inevitable in any old manuscript and is not considered serious unless it affects the text.

Damp-stained: Caused by moisture, damp-staining is an overall discoloration. It could make the paper limp and the writing slightly blurred.

Foxed (foxing): Foxing refers to scattered rust-colored spots caused by the paper's absorption of moisture.

Ink-burned: If a piece is ink-burned it means that the high acid content of the ink used has, over a period of time, actually eaten into the paper. Where the ink is heaviest there may be holes where the ink has eaten completely through.

Inlaid: The term *inlaid* indicates that the size of a manuscript, document, or letter has been altered by the addition of new paper. The new paper is frequently found as a very narrow (1/8″ to 1/4″) band expertly and discretely matched and attached around the four sides of a piece in order to improve its appearance or preserve the formerly tattered, torn, or discolored edges.

Mounted: A mounted item has been affixed to usually larger and thicker paper with an adhesive. Mounting is used as a means of preservation or to improve a piece's appearance; beware of early pieces mounted with glue that has stained or damaged the article.

Retouched where originally light: In the early days of autograph collecting, in order to preserve a manuscript, to increase its value, or to make it more legible, a later hand with fresh ink might have carefully traced over a piece's original writing. Retouching does decrease the value of a piece. If you have reason to believe retouching has been done, a good magnifying glass should answer your doubts.

Silked: A piece that has been "silked" has been preserved by being placed between two layers of gauze or other museum-type approved material to prevent the autograph material from completely deteriorating. The sheer material is usually professionally applied and affects the appearance only slightly if it has been applied skillfully. It may be added to an entire document or used only on a damaged area.

Spotted: Actual foreign material, solid or liquid, may sometimes fall on a piece, leaving the paper spotted. The spotting could be caused by coffee, tea, wine, or something from a little snack somebody was having the last time that article was inspected.

Tape-stained: A tape stain is the ugly brown stain that remains after the removal of older-type transparent tape. Nonstaining archival tape is now used quite safely.

Water-stained: Water staining is not caused merely by humidity or careless spotting. It usually covers large areas and results from actual immersion or partial immersion of the piece in water.

Worn along folds: Where a letter has been folded and unfolded over a long period of time the paper becomes thinned and sometimes separated.

Because the collecting of books, manuscripts, and autographs have begun to overlap, these terms are descriptive of the faults that any collector in a field dealing with paper could encounter. Some of these faults are unavoidable and do not depreciate the value of a collectible. Others are destructive and should be taken into account when you are buying or bidding. Generally speaking, a piece that is browned, inlaid, mounted, or silked does not depreciate much in value because of such a characteristic.

Photographs

Certainly, one of the most popular fields is collecting autographed photographs. While you can always collect the contemporary 8″ × 10″ glossy in color, it is amazing how far

This is the verso (back side) of a carte de visite photograph of fairy tale author *Hans Christian Andersen.* Andersen has written in Danish: "You Danish fresh seashore. The iron of the plough discovers the golden horn. God give you future, as he gave you memories. You I love, Denmark, the land of my fathers." Value: $1,450.

back in time you can go if you choose to collect older photographs, considering that photography is a relatively modern phenomenon. Two common forms of old photograph are the *carte de visite* and the *cabinet photograph.*

Overall measuring approximately 2 1/2″ × 4″, cartes de visite were produced by the thousands from around 1861 to 1866. The actual photo image was about 2 1/4″ × 3 1/2″ and was affixed to a larger stiff mount. The photographer's name could be printed on both the front and the back of the mount. The space below the image was often used for the autograph of the sitter, although many preferred to sign on the verso.

Following the popularity of the carte de visite, the larger cabinet photographs were introduced to the United States after success in Europe. The print measured about 4″ × 5 1/2″ and was mounted to a 4 1/4″ × 6 1/2″ card leaving a space at the foot where it could be signed. It, too, carried the photographer's usual artistic logo.

It is amazing how many world-famous personages were photographed and signed their photographs around and during the 1860s and the later nineteenth century. On record there are signed cabinet cards and carte de visite photos of Hans Christian Andersen,

Alexander Gustave Eiffel autographed this cabinet photograph only a few years after he had given the world his famed Eiffel Tower and the superstructure of The Statue of Liberty. Value: $950.

Louis Pasteur, Henrik Ibsen, Samuel F. B. Morse, members of European royalty, and early U.S. presidents, to mention just a few examples.

The terminologies and abbreviations listed in this chapter are *generally* accepted by collectors and dealers, but there is no standard or rule that everyone follows. Some dealers use periods after each letter in abbreviations, some use all capital letters, and some use only lowercase letters. Whatever the case, the abbreviations are a shorthand method of description and are used accordingly. For your own purposes you will probably make up a few of your own.

Evaluation

What makes *your* autograph letter worth more than *mine*? Even if we try to speak in terms of evaluation we end up speaking about price, because ultimately these terms blend. *Value, evaluation,* and *price* in autograph terms are going to be used hereafter interchangeably, almost synonymously, even if we know that the dictionary gives slightly different definitions for the terms.

While the advanced collector knows the justification for value, the novice and intermediate hobbyist is not necessarily aware of the nuances. The novice does not know the subtlety of why his or her letter was "cheap" and your letter is beyond his budget. But value, and consequently evaluation, is definitely bonded to price.

Investment and *Profit* Are Not Dirty Words

The purist in the field of philography takes exception to the suggestion of profit or the question, "How much is it worth?" *Investment* is also a dirty word. The idea that a hobby should conjure up in the minds of its participants thoughts of money horrifies a true purist. Most collectors face the fact, however, that the bits and pieces of paper they collect *do* have a monetary value which, in some cases, is quite considerable.

So despite the antagonism of some, we cannot overlook either the present or potential value of what we collect. No matter how much pleasure your collection brings, you must ultimately face the inevitability of its worth. Almost everything costs something, so let us not allow naïveté to make us believe that the *joy* of collecting should necessarily overshadow the price we pay for what we collect.

How many times have you heard that you should collect for the sheer delight it gives you or that you should never think of your hobby as an investment? Probably the only major expenditure we can all identify with in those noninvestment terms is the purchase of a car. Most people do not purchase a new (or used) automobile and think during the negotiations about what a great investment they are making.

If you were honest with yourself the last time you bought a car, you knew that the moment you signed the papers, put the key in the ignition, and drove off the lot you had already lost several hundred to several thousand dollars. (The exception, of course, would be the purchase of a classic, already-classic, or going-to-be-classic automobile.)

Do you buy stocks because they give you pleasure? Well, you might reply affirmatively if you actually took possession of them. Normally they are held in trust by the broker until you sell them, and you never have the opportunity to enjoy those beautifully engraved certificates. The answer to the question, therefore, is no!

You buy stocks to sell them for a profit. You might purchase real estate for a number of reasons, but your ultimate goal is profit. Even your home which you bought for immediate gratification (and shelter) must be considered a long-term investment on which you hope to make a profit. And, like it or not, underlying the joy of acquiring autographs is the concept of investment.

Autographs Have Value and Stability

There are collectibles on today's market that are utterly valueless. To expect a return on your investment when you have grown tired or bored with it would be more than optimistic.

Hobbies, like fads, come and go. However, acquiring autographs is hardly a fad. You can count Julius Caesar as an early collector. Philately (stamp collecting) is one of our most widespread and highly respected hobbies. Certainly art and book collecting fall into the same category of respectability. They are stable. That is to say, there is an open market for both buying and selling.

Due to the magic of the world's communication systems the growth of philography has been phenomenal. There are collectors in Daytona Beach, Florida, who buy from dealers in Seattle, Washington. California dealers are buying from Chicago dealers. London collectors are selling to North Carolina dealers. Tokyo material is being traded to Germany. French, Norwegian, Canadian, Belgian, and Italian inventories are being disbursed all over the world.

Fax machines provide immediate access and identification to anybody who requests it. Where a fax machine is not available, overnight delivery of material or photocopies is possible.

The point here is that because of the huge worldwide market that has been created

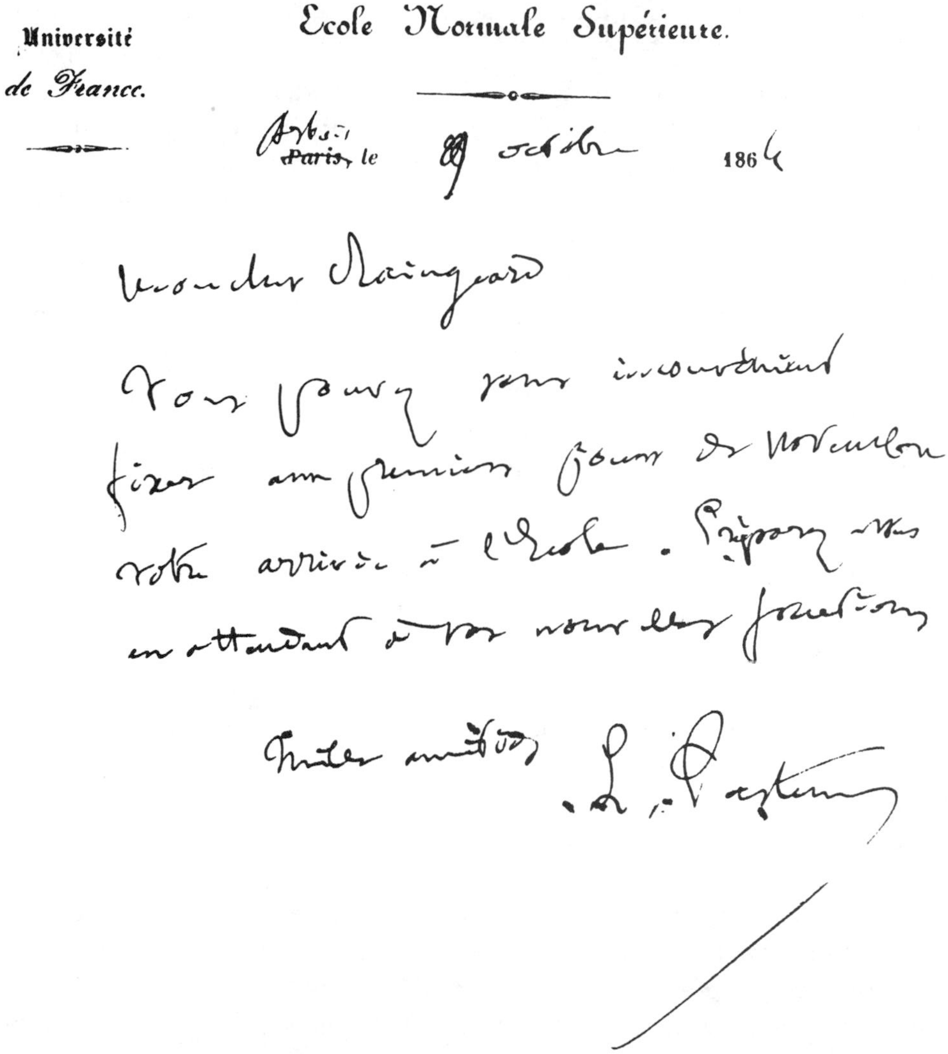

Université
de France.

École Normale Supérieure.

Arbois ~~Paris~~, le 9 octobre 1864

Mon cher Raingeard

Vous pouvez sans inconvénient fixer au premier jour de novembre votre arrivée à l'École. Préparez-vous en attendant à vos nouvelles fonctions.

Mille amitiés L. Pasteur

Louis Pasteur, the doctor and chemist whose name became part of our language, has also left us heir to his precious letters. Value: $2,500.

as the result of sophisticated telecommunications, the value of this collectible has accelerated proportionately. Stop to think of all the collectibles that do not have the ease of transportability that autographs possess. Think of those that are too large or too perishable to enclose in an envelope and send across this continent or to some other part of the world.

The International Aspect

Autograph collecting is now international. As farfetched as it may seem, your ability to understand currency exchange becomes important in evaluating your own collection.

For example, let us assume you were fortunate enough several years ago to have purchased a number of good British or French items, such as pieces signed by Dickens, Lord Horatio Nelson, Auguste Renoir, and Louis Pasteur, at the going rate of exchange when the dollar was high. If you were to sell them back to the same dealers today for the *same* price you originally paid for them in pounds or francs, you would make a very tidy profit in U.S. dollars. If you resold them overseas at a very modest markup, you would gain handsomely because those pieces have increased in value every year since their purchase.

This discussion is not an effort to make you into an international trader. It is a means of letting you know how vast the market has become and of giving you an idea of its versatility.

As you rate and value your material, consider also that values differ for similar or like autographs between the United States and Europe. The same is true between our East Coast and West Coast. This geographical factor is best exemplified by Civil War items, which command a premium in the South, and entertainment and movie autographs, which are valued more in the entertainment capitals of New York and California than in other parts of the country.

Values

Now that we have pointed out to you the national and international scope and the current growth of this industry, let's explore values and what affects them. The purpose of this chapter is not to quote prices that will ultimately be outdated, but rather to give you information that will be *permanently* useful. (Books such as our companion book, *The Price Guide to Autographs,* Wallace-Homestead, can aid you in buying and selling.)

The value (price) of an autograph is affected by many variables just as any commodity is, and, like any other commodity, not the least of these variables is *supply and demand.*

When there are lots of strawberries in the market during the summer, the price is low. When there are very few strawberries in the market in the middle of winter, the price is very high. And so it goes with any kind of produce. Further, if you have a tremendous supply of berries but too many customers, the price will rise. Inversely, if you have a very short supply of berries and an even shorter supply of customers, the price will fall. This concept works with bananas, cars, money, and autographs. It is the natural law of supply and demand.

Not too long ago—a very few years—you could hear conversations among collectors about what to buy. Should it be an Abraham Lincoln, a George Washington, a Robert E. Lee, or a Marilyn Monroe letter or document? Ah! Decisions, decisions! Today? Today you would be fortunate to find just a signature.

Yes, the hobby has grown that much and the demand has grown with it. Of course, letters and documents of very famous people are still available, but the cost is now many times what it was before because there are considerably more collectors bidding for fewer berries. But, you say, *everything* has gone up, including cars, houses, and food. True! The difference is that we can manufacture more cars, build more houses, and grow more food, but Abraham, George, Robert E., and Marilyn aren't signing any more documents or writing any more letters.

When a large autograph cache of one person is suddenly found, a temporary imbalance can be created. The imbalance is not necessarily harmful, however, depending on how the discovery is handled. There should be no panic if common sense prevails, but when you have paid several hundred or several thousand dollars for an item because of its rarity in the marketplace only to read the painful news that a large trunkful of similar material was found in an abandoned mine shaft in lower Frog Hop, Arkansas, your disappointment is unprintable.

Chances are it will never happen. If it does, the lucky discoverer of these possibly hundreds of items would most likely be discreet and intelligent enough not to "dump" them on the market in one large lot. Dumping would not only depreciate the value of *your* piece but would depreciate the discoverer's pieces as well. Instead, the clever discoverer would allow the pieces to be absorbed slowly over a large geographic area, thereby allowing the law of supply and demand to quietly adjust.

Case in point: Hundreds of canceled checks were sold by a private party to a dealer. These were personal checks of a very famous personality all signed in full. The going price prior to their discovery was approximately $225. Because some discernment was used in their disbursal, the price after the absorption remained the same.

Rarity

Rarity—what is it? All too often rarity is "in the eye of the beholder" or, frequently, in the eye of the cataloger. *Rarity* is a word with kaleidoscopic meaning when applied to autograph material, but certainly rarity, true rarity, is an essential factor in evaluation. The term does not necessarily denote how many of something *exist*. It can indicate how many are *available*.

If, through the years, certain autograph material has been gobbled up by public and university libraries, privately endowed libraries and historical societies, or wealthy col-

Approved, and ordered to be carried into effect.

A. Lincoln

Oct. 17, 1862.

Abraham Lincoln is perhaps America's most wanted president among autograph collectors. No presidential collection can be complete without an example of his signature and handwriting. Value: $3500–$4500.

lectors who will one day donate their collections to an institution, then what was once a common, easily available autograph item has now become rare only because it is no longer circulating throughout the philography market—even though there are actually thousands of pieces extant.

Consider rarity as being relative to what is available. Lincoln and Washington autograph material is not actually few in number, but the demand for such pieces is high. Consequently, they realize high prices.

We know that pieces from signer of the Declaration of Independence Button Gwinnett are rare, as are pieces from signer Thomas Lynch, Jr. These men made no significant historical contributions to the country *except* as signers. Their value as philographic rarities comes about because they both died as young men, leaving few examples of their autographs. The high prices their signatures command are not the result of their importance in the course of U.S. history. Their value is directly proportional to the number of collectors who would like to complete a set of all the signers.

Just as rare as is the signature of Button Gwinett is the collector who could afford to buy it. The heady atmosphere of high-priced material is where Mr. Gwinett has flown. Most experienced collectors, however, would likely place themselves on a far more conservative financial level.

Ratio of Values

Beginners would likely (and wisely) put themselves in the budget category. Whatever you are able to afford is out there, available, and you will find a courteous, interested dealer or collector to help you. Unlike other hobbies in which you may be high pressured into purchases you cannot afford, in autograph collecting you will discover that those from whom you buy more often than not have deep regrets about parting with a piece. They know there will never be another exactly like it.

Mary Benjamin, in her informative and knowledgeable 1966 edition of *Autographs: A Key to Collecting,* writes in regard to evaluating the ratio of the value of an L.S. to an A.L.S. to a D.S.:

Among the more stable and general rules which the dealer, and after him the majority of collectors, has learned, is a simple one applying to letters and documents considered as average. Among this type there is to be noted what can be called a relationship or ratio of values. The A.L.S., which is normally the most highly valued, is used as the basis in this comparison. If an A.L.S., for example, is worth $4, the following values will govern: An A.D.S. or an A.N.S. will be worth $3; an L.S., $2, and a D.S. $1.

This rule could safely be used in the valuing of autograph material prior to the twentieth century, but so many variables have entered the scene that these ratios do not now necessarily apply. Because the industry has grown so remarkably, creating specialists in so many divisions, the marketplace now dictates values. We are not going to debate *why* a signed photograph of a certain person in a particular section of collecting may demand a higher price than that person's autographed letter. Obviously, many collectors have been ''turned on'' to photographs, and the marketplace is telling us that in some categories pictures speak louder than words.

Content

Let us assume you are considering the purchase of a letter written by actor Dustin Hoffman and another by the long-deceased scientist Albert Einstein. What should be your priorities in establishing their values? The answer is *content.*

In either case, if, in the pieces under consideration, Mr. Hoffman or Professor Einstein wrote a formal acceptance to an invitation or a polite reply to an autograph request, the value is considerably less than if Dustin Hoffman wrote about his performance in his last Academy Award–winning film or Albert Einstein wrote about what contribution his theory of relativity made to mankind. Autograph items with interesting, relevant, pertinent, historical, or earth-shattering information are far more desirable, and, thus, more valuable, than pieces displaying mundane content. The premium you pay for good content is rarely wasted. The hypothetical pairing of two incongruous personalities in the example above is presented to emphasize the value of content in any category, be it entertainment or science. However, note that although Mr. Hoffman's letter with interesting content is more valuable than his routine letter, it will never equal the value of *either* of Professor Einstein's letters.

Interesting handwritten letters of prominent contemporary persons are valued more

March 19,1952

Hon.John S.Fine
Governor of Pennsylvania
Executive Offices
Harrisburg,Pa.

My dear Governor Fine:

　　　　Since mailing my letter of March 6th it came to my mind that there is another man who, according to my opinion, should be on the list of those invited to participate in the Aaronsburg project, namely Mr.James Warburg,New York City, who has written outstanding pamphlets and books concerning U.S.foreign policy.

　　　　　　Sincerely yours,

　　　　　　A. Einstein.

　　　　　　Albert Einstein.

Professor *Albert Einstein* usually refrained from dictating such letters of recommendation (especially in English rather than in German), but he made this exception on behalf of his brilliant colleague, James Warburg. Value: $3,000.

---

highly than those that are typewritten or dictated. Because people of importance no longer have the time it takes to dash off a penned (or even penciled) communication, prices are much higher for such pieces than for the mechanically produced variety. However, in general, a dictated letter with good content will take precedence over an A.L.S. of lesser content.

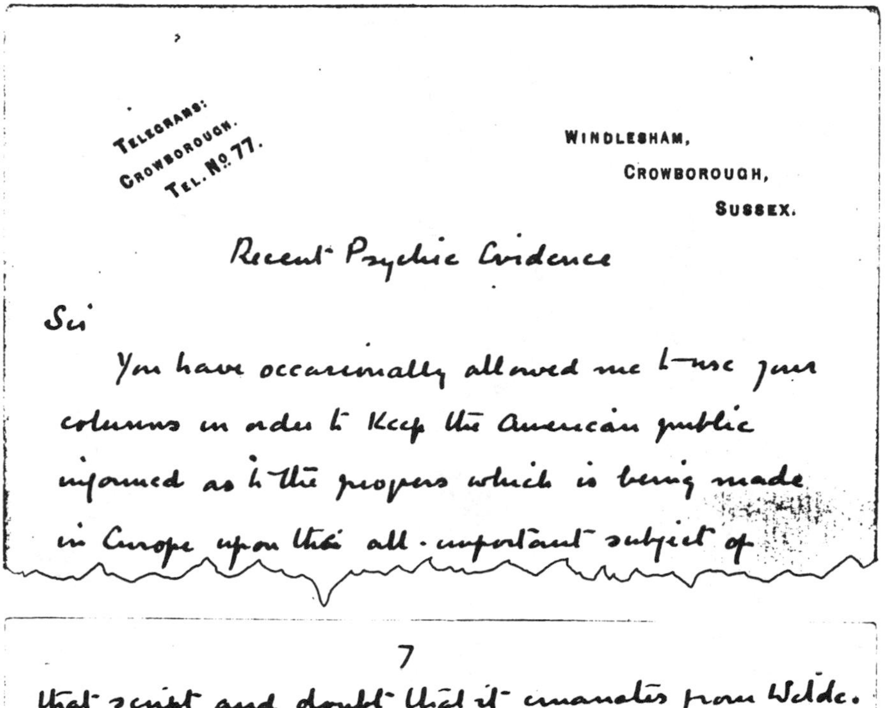

TELEGRAMS:
CROWBOROUGH.
TEL. No. 77.

WINDLESHAM,
CROWBOROUGH,
SUSSEX.

Recent Psychic Evidence

Sir

You have occasionally allowed me to use your columns in order to keep the American public informed as to the progress which is being made in Europe upon this all-important subject of

7

that script and doubt that it emanates from Wilde. One may imitate a man's features, one may forge his name, but it is impossible to sustain a deception in a prolonged communication from a great writer. Verily there is no sort of proof under heaven which has not been accorded to us, and those beyond must despair sometimes of ever penetrating our obtuse intelligence.

Yours faithfully

Arthur Conan Doyle.

The unusual content of this seven-page A.L.S. by *Sir Arthur Conan Doyle* makes it one of the rarest letters he ever penned. Value: $10,000.

Academy Award–winning actor *David Niven* was greeted backstage by Sanders just moments after the suave British actor accepted an Oscar in 1959 for his performance in "Separate Tables."

The Warner Brothers tough guy. *Humphrey Bogart's* rare signature, matted with a photo, is currently valued at $750. A signed photo would be worth much more.

Association Value

With so many divisions of autographs from which to choose, you should be aware that within whatever categories you are collecting, whether presidents, authors, artists, composers, aviators, etc., your piece has more value if an author is discussing literary matters or an aviator is writing about aeronautics. That would include one author writing to another author, artist to artist, and so on. In general, a presidential letter or document signed while the person was in office carries a higher price than a piece signed by that person at another time. Records show that one president writing to another president, or even referring to another, will enhance the value of the piece of writing.

Condition

Common sense tells you that anything in poor condition will bring less than the identical object in excellent condition. Although *pristine* is a favorite adjective among collectors, there are few legitimately pristine pieces. When you discover a truly rare item, do not

Samuel Goldwyn, co-founder of MGM and president of Samuel Goldwyn Studios for most of his life, talks with Sanders. The original doodles accompanying his signature make it even more valuable.

let its condition discourage you from purchasing it. Its value will be in its scarcity, not in its condition.

Paper, being what it is, is easily damaged. Most pieces with any age at all have been repeatedly handled, folded, and refolded. Those folds may show breaks or complete separations. Edges can be frayed or torn, and depending on where a piece has been stored, it can be stained or foxed. Fortunately, there are many excellent restorers, and many defects can be repaired very inexpensively.

There are also archival materials available to the collector who wants to mend minor flaws. Faded ink is one area where no one treads. *There is no known method of enhancing a faded document or letter.* Retrace the writing and you render it worthless because you have now entered the field of forgery.

Length

Who would ever believe that the one-page letter with content would command a premium over a two- or three-page letter with similar text? Once upon a time length was of no great importance in establishing value, but as the hobby grew it became popular to frame and display collected prizes. A two-page letter written on both sides of the page would have to be double-glassed in order to display the entire letter. An alternate to the single page would be a two-page letter written on the first and third sides of a double letter

George Sanders and Portland, Oregon, disc jockey Sammy Taylor backstage with *Jerry Lee Lewis* in the 1960s after Lewis had forsaken rock and roll music for country and western.

Rose Fitzgerald Kennedy, mother of a U.S. president and two U.S. senators, signs the Sanders guest book as George and his eldest son, "Sandy," look on.

sheet. As a consequence, a one-page letter with good content, suitable for framing, can be valued at anywhere from 25 percent to 50 percent more than its longer counterpart.

Are there exceptions? Of course there are. For example, a seven-page letter written by Sir Arthur Conan Doyle about a scientifically sponsored seance in which he describes the meeting and names the participating scientists is of tremendous value. A brief one-page version of this very detailed letter would not have the value of the seven-page account.

Conclusion

In our *The Price Guide to Autographs,* prices reflect the average marketplace value of average material in good condition with no special content or association. It is only a guide. Obviously, the collector, dealer, or auction house involved with your piece on the very day you buy, sell, or trade it becomes the final arbiter.

There is no finite value when it comes to an autograph. There is no sharp edge because of the infinite variety of material and of taste that dictates material's popularity. From year to year, country to country, category to category, the popularity of specific autograph material changes. There will always be some areas of collecting that are more popular than others and will, as a consequence, command higher prices even in times of economic stress. Follow where your interests lead, and do not worry too much about predicting long-term trends in autograph values.

Beware the Forger

Anyone can sign John Wayne's name on a photograph, and many do. A few years ago, we attended a Western movie memorabilia show. One of the dealers had a box of signed photos, with several by the immortal he-man neatly grouped. Fortunately, even a novice could see that these had been scribbled by different hands—at least one far too feminine to be the Duke's. Not one, by the way, was even close to authentic.

Authenticity is of prime concern to the collector. One reason why books like our own autograph price guide and other books which contain facsimiles are so popular is because of this concern. Using the most recent edition of *The Price Guide to Autographs*, for example, you could simply compare what is being offered to you as Wayne's signature to the one in the photograph in the book. One that matches is worth the approximate value stated in the guide. Otherwise, the value is zip, since there is little market for the clumsy forgeries of crooked flea market dealers.

Honest Mistakes

Nor are out-and-out forgeries the only thing to be alert about. Historical coincidence is another. There have been a great many men throughout the centuries named John Tyler, but only one was President of the United States. Signatures of the nonfamous John Tylers have little value, although they are certainly authentic signatures of John Tyler.

An even better example of the potential for honest confusion is the autograph of the two Winston Churchills. Sir Winston, of course, was the leader of the British Empire during War War II, the very epitome of a cigar-chomping English bulldog. Sir Winston was born in 1874. However, *another* Winston Churchill, an American, was born in 1871, and his life somewhat paralleled that of the British Churchill. The American Winston

Legendary *John Wayne* during a television broadcast with Sanders in 1959. Wayne's autograph is now one of the most difficult to acquire, and many forgeries have surfaced in recent years.

Dec 26. 1917.

Dear Mr Speaker
Many thanks for your letter about
the ruins at Carrock & Lazscale,
as to which I am at once
making inquiries.

Yours sincerely.
Winston S. Churchill

The autograph of British prime minister *Winston S. Churchill,* is still in great demand by autograph collectors. Value: $1,700.

Churchill was, in his time, a popular author of historical novels about the political and economic issues of his day. He had a wide following, and the name of one of his most memorable characters, Jethro Tull, has been used as the name of a popular rock group.

Both Churchills were writers and both wrote about political topics. There are numerous autographed books extant by both. The difference in value is about $10 for a product of Churchill the American as opposed to $400 or more for a product of Churchill the Englishman. Both autographs are authentic, you just have to research which is which and know what you are buying.

In other words, the more knowledge that you have, the less likely it is that you will be taken in by an "autograph of mistake." You can never know too much or have too large a reference library.

Secretarial Signatures

It has been common practice for very busy people to have their secretaries answer and sign routine mail. This is especially true in the movie industry, where even back in the twenties the studios sometimes maintained banks of people who did nothing but sign stars' names on photographs and letters.

A secretarial autograph of John Wayne is worth about the same as one perpetrated by the crooked flea market dealer mentioned above—nada, nothing, zip. The answer, of course, is to consult a facsimile book and compare the piece against a known authentic signature.

Secretarial autographs are not attempts at out-and-out forgeries. The name of the famous personage is usually simply signed in whatever hand the secretary may possess. Thus, they are normally easy to detect by comparison.

Expert Help

To this point, we've talked about forgeries that are obvious to any collector (assuming he or she has access to authentic comparison facsimiles like those in many price guides and references). There are and always have been, however, forgers of considerable talent throughout the ages who can fool even experts some of the time. Museums have paintings by unknown forgers hanging on their walls, purporting to be Old Masters. Occasionally, one of these is unmasked, bringing much embarrassment to the museum's curator.

The same holds true in the autograph field. Chance of forgery is the reason for getting a lifetime guarantee on pieces you buy from an autograph dealer. Legitimate dealers will gladly provide such a guarantee—which means, should a piece be proven to be a forgery three years from now, you get your money back. Such guarantees place pressure on the dealer to consult with experts and make sure that autographed items are authentic. *Ask dealers to tell you who they do business with and what their methods of authentication are.*

Well-executed forgeries require painstaking and extremely thorough examination by experts to expose. Special equipment and a knowledge of characteristics of forged and genuine writing are needed. Correct methods of comparing handwriting must be used. Knowledge of types of paper prevalent during different historical periods and other such background is a must.

Kenneth W. Rendell, writing in *Autograph and Manuscripts* (Scribner's, 1978), details the equipment and procedures for detecting forgeries. A microscope of variable power ($10\times$–$100\times$), with a special holder for documents, is one of the most important instruments in the authentication expert's arsenal. Considerable time is spent by the expert in closely comparing samples of writing. Obviously, such time-consuming and knowledge-dependent techniques are beyond (dare we say) the scope of most of us. If there is any doubt at all about a piece, seek out a recognized authentication expert.

The Autopen

Writing to a famous person (especially a politician) and receiving a signed letter in return is quite easy. Only, chances are, the signature was done by an automatic signature machine (the most common brand is the Autopen). Such signatures are worth very little indeed compared to an actual autograph.

In the case of politicians, for the most part they are just too busy and receive too much correspondence to send the average person a personally signed letter. Take President Bush as an example. The White House mailbag brings in hundreds of letters a day. There is no possible way the President could actually read all his mail, much less dictate and sign all the replies that go out in his name. Machines do it. The note that comes back to you may look like it was typed by a secretary and then signed by the Chief Executive, but the technological marvels of a word processor and an Autopen really generated the letter.

All presidents, from John F. Kennedy on, have relied extensively on this method to satisfy the enormous demands for their autographs. Congress members, senators, cabinet officers, and (more recently) Supreme Court Justices have taken to this technology with a vengeance. In a way, since our tax dollars buy these automatic signature devices, the American taxpayer is subsidizing forgery.

"Within four or five square blocks [in downtown Washington] you've got more people who need [Autopens] than anyplace else in the world," Robert DeShazo said in an article by Lynne Cheney published in the *Washingtonian* magazine. DeShazo is president of the International Autopen Company, which is the major manufacturer of automatic signature machines.

Using a mechanical device to duplicate signatures in specific and writing in general goes back many hundreds of years. Those who have had the fortune to visit Thomas Jefferson's home Monticello (near Charlottesville, Virginia) have seen such a device on display there. Jefferson's "polygraph" was the eighteenth-century equivalent of the photocopy machine. As Jefferson wrote with one pen, another (which was mechanically attached to the first) created an exact copy. It was moderately simple mechanically and works as well today as it did back then. Jefferson, as evidenced by this machine and the other wondrous devices in his palatial home, was an avid gadgeteer. If he were alive today, his office would no doubt boast a thousand-watt-per-channel state-of-the-art stereo and a personal computer system that could do everything but brush his teeth (and maybe that too!)

That supreme nineteenth-century showman, P. T. Barnum, went even further. He had a machine that could sign his signature in his absence—one of the first true automatic signature machines. With a sucker being born every minute, Barnum evidently felt he needed help in corresponding with them.

Still, despite the machines existing, no U.S. president felt the need for one until John F. Kennedy took office in 1961. This does not mean that earlier presidential autographs are all signed in the actual hand of that president. Many were signed by secretaries and fall under the classification of "secretarial."

President Kennedy and his staff, naturally, did not go around telling autograph collectors that a machine was doing much of the President's work for him, but certain astute collectors soon became suspicious. The giveaway is that many of Kennedy's signatures, held up in pairs to a light, can be *exactly* superimposed on each other. The odds against anyone signing his or her name that precisely every time are astronomic. We humans are simply not that precise.

Noted expert Charles Hamilton, who has meant so much to the world of autograph collecting, warned on the "Today" show during the Kennedy administration of the possible "grave consequences" of presidential Autopen usage. Pierre Salinger, Kennedy's press secretary, immediately denied that such a device was in the White House.

Hamilton, however, followed his television appearance by demonstrating that there were not one but seven patterns being used by the machine to duplicate JFK signatures. Several of them were "John Kennedy," but there was also a "Jack Kennedy" to be used on letters to his friends.

Lyndon Johnson, who was too busy pulling his beagle's ears (for which some of us will never forgive him), took to the Autopen even more enthusiastically. The late Jennifer Casoni—an autograph dealer in Alexandria, Virginia—even maintained that Johnson used the Autopen to sign his vice-presidential oath of office!

Richard Nixon continued the Autopen tradition. Casoni, in her book *Best Wishes, Richard Nixon,* identified nine "Richard Nixon" patterns and three "R.N." patterns. The Nixon White House, as previous administrations, was reluctant to admit the use of this automatic signing device.

President Gerald Ford gets credit for honesty in this respect. He was the first president to own up to Autopen usage. In fact, to the surprise of the autograph collecting world, requests for autographs were often replied to with an Autopen signature and a letter stating that it was such a signature. In fact, the combination of these two have some small value just for their historical precedent of presidential honesty.

Jimmy Carter also used the Autopen extensively. These mechanical Carter signatures are relatively easy to detect when compared against known patterns. But Carter also made extensive use of the "secretarial" signature, which irritates collectors a good deal more than the more obvious Autopen signature because it is often very difficult to detect. Herman Darvick, a leading autograph expert and auction gallery owner, says that Susan Clough, a Carter secretary, "forged his name beautifully." While many presidents have countenanced this type of "forgery," Carter's usage of it has been very frustrating to collectors because such signatures turn up in places where they shouldn't.

"I saw a picture," Darvick said, "signed by Begin and Sadat, which was sent to

To George Sanders with appreciation for his friendship and best wishes from Dick Nixon.

Iranian ambassador Nouri Amjani and George Sanders listen intently to President *Richard M. Nixon* as he explains foreign policy problems in the Middle East.

73

Color photographs such as this one (shown here in black-and-white) signed by three of the presidents pictured are now valued at $1,000; when signed by all four men in the picture, the photographs are valued at $3,500.

the White House for Carter's signature. Susan Clough signed it for him. The Autopen would have been better—at least it would have been his real signature, even if a machine produced it.''

The Reagan White House was as anxious to discuss the use of the Autopen as it was to talk about what Ollie North did or did not do. Still, experts agree that approximately a dozen patterns were used to produce President Reagan's signature. There is a ''Ronald Reagan,'' a ''Ron,'' a ''Ronnie,'' and a ''Dutch.'' There is also an Autopen pattern of ''Ronald Reagan'' and ''Nancy Reagan'' together, given away by the fact that both signatures are on the exact same level, a physical impossibility in a normal signing by two individuals.

If you sent President George Bush a letter congratulating him on the capture of Manuel Noriega or on some other feat, the response that came back from the White House might *appear* to have been signed by the President himself; however, you could be sure that the real signer was the trusty Autopen.

Robert DeShazo, president of the International Autopen Company, has been manufacturing Autopen devices since 1942. We spoke with him in researching this subject recently, and he very kindly gave us some insight into the use of Autopens from the viewpoint of the public figure.

The average person, Mr. DeShazo explained, has no comprehension of the vast amount of mail received by prominent public figures, and thus little understanding or acceptance of the need for the machines his company provides. Since personal response to each and every letter is physically impossible, it is far better for an Autopen response to be generated than for the correspondent to be simply ignored.

Located in Sterling, Virginia, DeShazo's company ships Autopens all over the world. However, the company's proximity to Washington, D.C., is no accident.

"Almost every member of the Senate has one," he said. The House of Representatives is well stocked with Autopens also, though DeShazo added that sometimes four or five members might share one machine. In all, he estimated that over 500 Autopens are in use in Washington alone, to the disgust of autograph collectors but the relief of public officials facing literal mountains of correspondence.

International Autopen currently has two popular models on the market. The Autopen 80 resembles a small desk with metal arms and springs on the left side of its surface. A pen is screwed into the end of a metal arm. The operator places letters or books or whatever beneath the pen. The machine produces about 300 signatures per hour. Since a standard ink pen is used, the signature looks authentic to the uninitiated.

Inside the desklike structure of the Autopen 80 is the revolving matrix which guides the pen. This matrix looks something like a large boomerang. It is cut according to the sample signature supplied by the customer. The matrix is easily changed to produce another version of the signature, or that of another person. The machine costs about $3,000, with each matrix selling for around $100. A more expensive model of the Autopen—costing around $10,000—adds automatic paper feed and other features to increase productivity.

International Autopen has dominated the automatic signing market for many years. Competition has surfaced from time to time. A complex electronic device called the Signa-Signer is one competitor, but the simpler Autopen continues to be the machine of choice at the moment.

Determining whether or not an autograph in your possession, or one under consideration for purchase, is genuine or Autopen-generated takes a modicum of detective work. Comparison is the hot tip here. That's why so many hundreds of authentic signatures are included in this book and in other guides.

It is also a good idea, in the case of celebrity signatures done since the advent of the Autopen (i.e., within the last 30 years at least), to have some known Autopen examples as a guide. One reference for this is the book *Seeing Double* by Marvin B. Blatt and

Norman Schwab (La-La Ltd, P.O. Box 2060, North Babylon, NY 11703; published in 1986). Blatt and Schwab's book contains over 250 facsimiles of Autopen signatures, including variants.

A key to using such a reference is to realize that an example does not have to superimpose exactly 100 percent to be identified as an Autopen pattern. If the paper was moved while the Autopen was signing, either deliberately or through mechanical slippage, minor variations can be induced. Still, putting a suspected piece over a known Autopen and moving the signatures around while holding them up to a strong light will cause parts of the signatures to match. No one can sign his or her name exactly alike twice in a row, so even if just sections of the two signatures match, the signature being investigated is almost certainly Autopen-generated.

There are only two ways you can really be sure that a signature was done using an Autopen. The first is to match it to a known Autopen example. The second is if you have two signatures that match exactly. Again, it's a physical impossibility for any person to sign his or her name precisely the same way twice; hence any two signatures that superimpose exactly were created by Autopen or by some other means of mechanical or electronic reproduction.

The Autopen and the newer technology of laser printers coming onto the market are a fact of life for the autograph collector. Knowledge is your only real protection. Seeing a current celebrity actually signing the piece in person is the only fool-proof guard against a signature's being produced by an Autopen or similar device. The second best and more practical way of assuring one-of-a-kind authenticity is dealing with a reputable dealer who can knowledgeably attest to a piece's authenticity or provide provenance (for example, a photograph of a book being signed by a famous author for the person now selling it).

Laser Printers

The new laser printer technology is the latest challenger for the automatic signing business, being able to produce a signature that looks very much like a handwritten one. With this device attached to a personal computer and a desktop publishing program, letters can be generated that incorporate "signatures" in a one-step process. In fact, there will very soon come a time when an Autopen signature will be considered a "personal" touch.

What Should You Collect?

Unlike so many other collectible hobbies, the acquisition of autographs is nearly unlimited in scope, categories, general interest, and availability. Just as the tastes and enthusiasms of human beings seem to be kaleidoscopic, so too are the possibilities in the collector's decision regarding what he or she decides to collect.

Collect What You Like

As you will soon discover, the various categories of autograph collecting are limited only by one's own personal interest in a certain group of people or type of person. For example, if you are particularly captivated by the work of artists who paint beautiful pictures, then it is possible that you might enjoy acquiring some of the artists' letters and documents, or even some of their signed sketches from old workbooks or meandering doodles scrawled on scrap paper.

The decision as to the type of artist to focus on is the next choice. Will you collect the signatures or writings of modernists, cubists, oil painters, water colorists, expressionists, American, German, French, English, Italian, or Ethiopian? Will the collection you plan on developing be general or specific? Such decisions are strictly up to you.

No future collector should be limited in this wide-ranging hobby by the suggestions, likes, or dislikes of spouses, companions, or trusted friends. This is going to be *your* hobby, and it will always reflect your personal curiosity and your willingness to devote contented hours, diligent effort, and even personal investment in an area that will pique your special interest.

You must think carefully about the type or types of celebrities whose pen or pencil scratchings will bring you joy and proud satisfaction, even inspiration. Once you've made that all-important decision, autograph collecting immediately becomes the treasure hunt of your lifetime. It is never-ending and never void of new and exciting possibilities.

Obviously, the way to end up with the opposite of all the previously described enthusiasm is to select an area of autograph collecting that is either boring or lacking in challenge. That possibility seems too needlessly senseless to pursue here, but it often happens to the unsuspecting collector who unwittingly listens to friends or family regarding the topic of specialization for this versatile hobby. One does not collect anything to satisfy the whims or preferences of others. The individual collector must make the ultimate decision and know that the choice will never bring anything but intellectual rewards, probably financial growth, and much personal satisfaction.

Categories of Collecting

There are over 30 general categories of collectible autographs listed in *The Price Guide to Autographs;* under these categories are listed over 15,000 individual names of celebrated and even infamous notables whose autographs are actually available to the collector. That number gives you some idea of the range this particular hobby enjoys. Considering that new celebrities are developing every day on this crowded planet of ours, the possibilities for new additions for your collection are virtually unlimited.

Mailing Requests to Celebrities

At this point you are probably wondering what all of this is going to cost. If you decide, as so many collectors do, that you would enjoy writing personal requests to contemporary celebrities in the area of interest you have selected as your favorite, then your costs will be modest. You will require postage and proper return envelopes or packaging for signed photographs or letters, and you will probably encounter a few other negligible charges.

The letter you address to a famous stranger will have to be interesting enough to inspire a willing reply. He or she receives hundreds of such requests from other collectors, so your message must be well thought out, polite, humbly challenging, and *brief!* Most important, it must include a self-addressed, stamped envelope or package for its return to you.

You should never, under any circumstances, rudely assume that the various celebrities to whom you write should return material to you at their personal expense. In most cases, they do not furnish unsigned photographs, typescripts, or personal memorabilia— *you* do! If a celebrity chooses to address a simple reply on his or her own stationery, be grateful, and don't expect that person to supply the postage stamp for the envelope. Those postal charges are always yours. Postal charges are the least you can expect to pay for such an autographic treasure. (A more detailed discussion of this method of collecting appears in Chapter 8.)

Buying Autographs

Many of our readers will not be interested in addressing ingenious pleas for autographs to contemporary notables, as they may have neither the time nor inclination for such pursuits. Such collectors prefer studying autograph dealers' catalogs and lists that are published and mailed to interested collectors at regular intervals throughout each year.

There are over 100 respectable autograph dealers functioning on a regular basis all over the United States, Great Britain, Sweden, Norway, West Germany, Japan, and in at least 15 other nations around the world. Thoroughly reputable auction houses also offer richly illustrated catalogs featuring autographs of the very celebrities and historically notable people you are attempting to collect.

In short, there are numerous sellers of autograph material for this fast-growing hobby, and you will ultimately discover just the right dealer for your specific needs. However, as is the case in all hobbies, determine up front just how much money you can conveniently afford to invest without disturbing, in any way, the security and current lifestyle of yourself and your family. The collector is frequently consumed by this exciting hobby and must be wary of financial pitfalls caused by the desire of wanting everything that is available for sale.

Budgeting Your Hobby

Before you begin, it is certainly wise to establish a budget for your purchases and *never,* under any circumstances, deviate from that sensible course. There will always be some item that you simply must have, but, unless you have unlimited funds, let pecuniary caution be your constant guide. As a wise owner of a chain of southern U.S. autograph galleries recently said, "There never is enough money to acquire all that we see that is actually available." That gallery owner, who has thousands of dollars to spend budgeted for the supplying of his business inventory needs, readily admits that *he* can't have it all, and the average collector faces a similar fate—on a different scale. In other words, set goals and potential costs in advance and try never to overspend.

You will find material available at every imaginable price range, and depending upon the category you have selected as your primary area of interest, there is usually something for every wallet or purse. There are dealers who offer only the rarest and most expensive material, and there are those who feature thousands of inexpensive but interesting items. The choice is always yours.

Dr. Sigmund Freud's letters are coveted by thousands of the world's serious autograph collectors. This example has a value of $3,000 to $4,000.

Setting Goals

You must never set impossible goals. For example, let us suppose you have decided to collect autographs of men and women of science. You probably will not be able to begin your collection with a meaningful letter signed by Sigmund Freud or Albert Einstein, as they are both relatively uncommon and obviously expensive. However, there are numerous Nobel prize winners in science and countless other scientific notables whose material is readily available at reasonable prices. In fact, many scientists will happily reply to a personal request for a signature if they find your letter courteous and thoughtful. Hence, you can begin your collection slowly and wisely. Acquiring good names, informative letters, and even signed photographs should be done with a sound sense of reasonable investment.

As you become more experienced and discover a particular autograph dealer with whom you sincerely enjoy dealing, you can begin your endless search for the Einstein or Freud piece—or their equals in your area of interest—that will become the prime source of pride in your autograph collection.

In this hobby, never permit yourself to be caught up in high-pressure tactics or uncontrollable impulse buying. If your budget does not allow for an overly expensive purchase this month or this year, be patient and wait until the desired autographic piece is a comfortable addition to your collection. Most autograph dealers are sincerely helpful and will not encourage you to overspend. In fact, frequently they will suggest or offer a less expensive item that will generally meet with your requirements. Some dealers even offer helpful layaway plans, and others now accept credit card payment.

Today's dealer does not need to push a rarity, such as a Freud, an Einstein, a George Washington, an Abraham Lincoln, or a Greta Garbo, as there are hardly enough of such items to satisfy customers' requests. Hence, every honest dealer is really attempting to fulfill your specified requirements with sound investment expertise and a professional eye upon your ultimate goals as a collector of worthwhile material.

Patience—Both a Virtue and a Necessity

Of course, as we mentioned earlier in this chapter, it is your own responsibility not to set impossible goals. One does not create a worthwhile collection of anything by attempting to "have it all" in the first few years of collecting. As we've already indicated, patience is the overriding key to collecting.

An impatient collector is frequently a careless overspender with more cash than brains. Such an impatient person makes unfortunate purchases of overpriced material and is awed only by big-name items that he or she hopes will impress his or her friends. Autograph collecting is fun and it can be impressive, but it should primarily be impressive to the owner and not to the friends, family, or acquaintances who may or may not "ooh" and "aah" over various additions to the collection.

If you are considering acquiring autographs as a hobby to impress your friends or business associates, you should instead raise thoroughbred racehorses, collect precious gems from Tiffany's, or buy classic Bugattis or oil paintings by the Old Masters, because your friends may not respond as enthusiastically to a lovely letter from the pen of Elizabeth Browning or Erma Bombeck. Your collection must satisfy *you*, not your visitors. Your collection is to be fun and relaxing for you; you should not collect autographs to titillate dear Aunt Alyce or cousin Gemma. This is your hobby and not some barometer of your wealth or success.

You cannot expect to assemble one of the most important collections in the world in a chosen area of expertise without studying all of the possibilities and utilizing your normal good sense during a quite lengthy period of your lifetime. However, on the way to such a lofty goal—or even a modest goal—you will find this hobby so rewarding that it can seem like Christmas or Hanukkah every day. New catalogs weekly, new autographs

Hope you're having good weather —

My love —

Grace —

A broadcaster for numerous Hollywood movie premieres, Sanders here shares his microphone with Academy Award–winning actress *Grace Kelly* a year before she became Princess of Monaco.

to be received regularly, new challenges daily. It is truly exciting and thoroughly satisfying as a hobby or an investment or both.

However, never lose sight of the fact that it is only a hobby and should be entertaining and relaxing. Overspend and it naturally becomes a pressurizing hardship. The financial budget you set should be only what you can comfortably afford without creating financial problems of any sort. It can be 5 percent or 10 percent of your spendable capital, or considerably more or less, depending upon your specific cash situation.

Most autograph dealers do not offer credit, and they expect to receive payment for their autographic offerings before forwarding them to you. It is customarily a cash in advance business, with rare exception. Classic or rare material has for years been a worthwhile investment, and you must cautiously consider that factor when you are paying today's relatively high prices (as opposed to those paid 10 or 15 years ago) for distinctive autograph material.

Who Collects?

It is our experience that collectors in this hobby are from all walks of life. We deal with physicians, attorneys, architects, actresses and actors, accountants, teachers, artists, truck drivers, security guards, blue-collar and white-collar workers. There are wealthy collectors and low-income collectors. They seem to come in all sizes and types.

Most are generally very nice, and the majority have that special quality that sets them apart: *curiosity*. They really want to know Grace Kelly's premarital secrets; yearn to understand Greta Garbo's insatiable desire for total privacy; wonder at the maniacal arrogance of Nazi leaders and the population who raised their arms to salute such men; laugh at Sir Charlie Chaplin's whimsical notes and caricatures; enjoy Enrico Caruso's

CHARLES CHAPLIN

May 21st, 1965

Dear Mrs Stock,

Thank you very much for your kind letter which made me very happy.

Yours sincerely

The autograph of "The Little Tramp" who became Sir Charles Chaplin (better known as *Charlie Chaplin*) continues to be a popular choice among autograph collectors. Value: $350.

and Houdini's worthwhile attempts at self-portraiture; thrive on uncovering nationally known politicians' juicy gossip about one another; burn to discover secrets contained in the available documents of various international heads of state. In short, collectors collect, and none do it better than those who consider autograph collecting as being the best of all possible hobbies.

A "Scattergun" Approach Doesn't Work

Unfortunately, one cannot employ the "scattergun" approach to collecting bits of history. So much material is available in so many categories that it will behoove the newcomer to consider the specialization we have alluded to earlier in this chapter. It is difficult to collect simply *everything,* and terribly confusing as well. You should specialize in a category or categories for as long as interest remains for you in those areas, and then, when your collection or a part of it seems satisfactorily complete to you, you should move on to some possibly related area.

As an autograph collector you will never be able to discontinue your search for knowledge. The hobby demands scholarly pursuits in researching and in acquiring a firm understanding of the material you collect. It will follow that you will insist on knowing minute details regarding the lives, careers, ambitions, desires, goals, and achievements of the notables whose papers you seek to own.

You orginally sought to possess a piece of paper mailed or discarded by a person

CUSHING ROAD
THOMASTON, MAINE

Sept. 17, 1965

Dear Mr. Butterman:

I have just received your letter with the 1965 wisdom Award of Honor scroll —

I am deeply honored by being chosen by your board of Editors —

With warmest thanks for your interest in my career

Sincerely yours,

Andrew Wyeth

Artist *Andrew Wyeth* is not famous for the letters he hates to write. Such an A.L.S. is valued at over $850.

of note because of your interest in that person. That interest grows each time you are able to hold in your hands something he or she once penned words onto, smiled or frowned down upon, and left fingerprints upon. You'll think about the fact that that person's prints are now being smothered by your own hands, and you'll feel that much closer to the author of each page you own. Yes, learn as you grow and never cease growing intellectually as there is much to learn in this hobby. To help you learn, we have listed at the end of this chapter some of the more important books available for your general study and research. Most are available from publishers or in public libraries.

For the totally uninformed but potentially serious autograph collector, here are some categories of collectibility that may catch your fancy. Consider collecting U.S. and foreign air aces; artists; photographers; authors; aviation pioneers; baseball, basketball, boxing, golf, and football stars; business and industry leaders; creators of well-known trademarks (inventors of household products and founders of famous companies); cartoonists and illustrators; Civil War leaders; composers; country music stars; Jewish figures; entertainers (contemporary and vintage); Olympic stars and other general sports celebrities; heads of state; governors of U.S. states; military leaders; Revolutionary War dignitaries

Mrs. Ruth Handler, co-founder and president of Mattel Toys, is interviewed by Sanders in 1952. A few years later, Mrs. Handler created the Barbie doll (named for her daughter) and became one of the world's wealthiest women.

Cordially yours,

Donald W. Douglas
President

Surrounded by models of his 1951 production planes, aircraft tycoon *Donald W. Douglas, Sr.* (center) prepares for his television debut. His son, who later became president of Douglas Aircraft Corp., and Sanders are shown also.

New York sports announcer Ted Husing, George Sanders, and Olympic decathlon gold medalist *Bob Mathias* (who later became a member of the U.S. Congress).

Happy holidays to you and yours.

Sincerely,

On the air with famed news commentator and syndicated newspaper columnist *Paul Harvey* in the 1960s. The letter to Sanders is recent—1989.

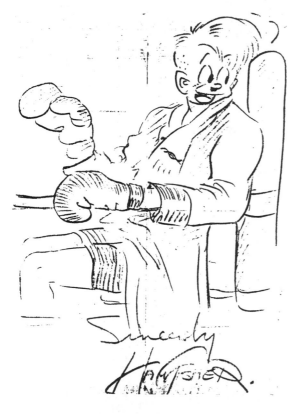

Roy Rogers and Trigger during a Hollywood charity event. George claims he not only got Roy's autograph but also got a hoofprint of the famous horse.

An original sketch of "Joe Palooka" by *Ham Fisher*.

and soldiers; rock music stars; pioneers in science and technology; clergy; and last, but certainly not least, U.S. presidents and their vice presidents.

Of course there are dozens of categories not listed above, including, perhaps, the one in which you have the most knowledge and the one you've already decided to begin your collection with. We sincerely welcome all facets of autograph collecting and are eager to learn of your discoveries.

Popular Hollywood organist *Korla Pandit*, actress-singer-author Helen Sanders, and cowboy singer *Doye O'Dell* appeared regularly on televsion in the early 1950s.

Singer *Lena Horne* listens intently to Sanders during an interview in New York for his syndicated "Sanders Meanders" program in the 1970s.

I hereby authorize and direct the Secretary of State to affix the Seal of the United States to remaining portion of imprisonment fine and costs, imposed upon Jason Mahan, for counterfeiting the silver coins of the U. States by the U. S. Circuit Court for the Eastern District of Pennsylvania. —
dated this day, and signed by me; and for so doing this shall be his warrant.

James K. Polk

Washington, December 19, 1844.

He may not have been a highly memorable president, but thousands of collectors want at least one written example from each U.S. president, and thus pieces by *James K. Polk* are becoming rarer by the minute. Value: $1,000.

Another U.S. president whose autographs have become expensive because of supply and demand is *Zachary Taylor*. Documents such as this one have $1,000 price tags.

Even a routine *Martin Van Buren* A.L.S like this one can command a price of $700.

The letters of *Ulysses S. Grant* range in price from $1,200 to $1,500, depending upon content.

A letter by President James Buchanan. Value: $1,150.

Important Collections—Yours and Malcolm's

Some collections are more important than others. The priceless collections of autograph material on display at the Huntington Library in San Marino, California, the breathtaking collection at the J. P. Morgan mansion in Manhattan, and the fabled holdings of the late publisher Malcolm Forbes are all extremely important collections.

However, all substantive autograph holders are "important" because they retain, protect, and display some of our most important history. Without such collections, vast numbers of historically important pieces of paper would be scattered to the proverbial winds. It is collectors who meticulously ward off damaging sunlight, voracious silverfish, mildew, and rust. It is collectors, like you, who will save for posterity the written treasures that might have been lost. Yours probably will not become the most extensive or ex-

55 Irving Place

N.Y. 4/3

My Dear Mr. Young

I won't be able to attend your friend's gathering on Saturday evening, owing to the engagement that I mentioned to you. Hope you have a good time

Your's Own truly

Sydney Porter

A piece by author *Sydney Porter,* alias O. Henry, a popular American writer. Such an A.L.S. may be priced as high as $1,200.

This first edition of **A FABLE,** printed on rag paper, is limited to

one thousand copies, signed by the author.

William Faulkner

NUMBER 861

Signed first and special editions are another source of treasures. This book is signed by author *William Faulkner.*

Pacific Grove, Calif
Oct 25 1948

Dear Mr. Seward:

Thank you for your very kind letter. I am sorry I have neither books nor pictures. The first I do not have around and the second I do not like.

Please don't make your students read my work. This could give them a hatred they would never out grow. If you want them to read my work - forbid it. Then they will not only read it but will have a fine sense of sin too and some triumph over authority.

Again thank you for your pleasant letter

Sincerely
John Steinbeck

Amazing modesty and cunning are illustrated by author *John Steinbeck* in this wonderful A.L.S. Value: $3,000.

Autographed photographs of *Thomas Edison* are uncommon and are in great demand. Value: $1,000.

pensive collection ever, but, with the proper selectivity, it can become a highly worthwhile gathering of history's footsteps—or hand prints.

Furthermore, your collection will mirror your personality and personal interests. Your efforts will make your collection important to you and possibly even to your progeny. As an investment, if you choose to acquire excellent and extraordinary material, it can be the best financial involvement you've ever had, including gold, real estate, precious jewels, and the seldom reliable stock market. That will be entirely up to you and your careful research.

Box 95,
Oteen, N. C.
August 9, 1937.

Miss Isabell Logan,
c/o Charles B Brooks,
Box 624,
Candler, N. C.

Dear Miss Logan:

Thanks very much for your very nice letter. Of course,
I shall be delighted to autograph your books and if I only
had more time and were more conveniently located, I should be
delighted to talk with you. I think that is going to be a
little difficult.

I am living in a cabin several miles outside of Asheville. There have been a lot of interruptions and I am trying
with all my might and main to push on with my work. If you
could come up sometime with some friend or member of your
family when I am not working, of course I should be glad to
talk with you. The best time would be around six o'clock
in the afternoon.

Meanwhile, if you will take your books and leave them
at the home of my Mother, Mrs. Julia E. Wolfe, 48 Spruce
Street, Asheville, I shall be delighted to autograph them
when I come in in a few days. Then you could pick them up
later. My address is Oteen, N. C., and if you would drop
me a card there, letting me know what you are going to do,
I would appreciate it.

Meanwhile, again thanks for your very nice letter and
with all good wishes,

Sincerely,

Thomas Wolfe

TW/veh

Author *Thomas Wolfe* preached that "you can never go back," but his letters have helped us to
do that. An interesting T.L.S. like this one will sell for nearly $2,000.

President *John F. Kennedy* provided an exclusive interview for Sanders's television and radio audiences.

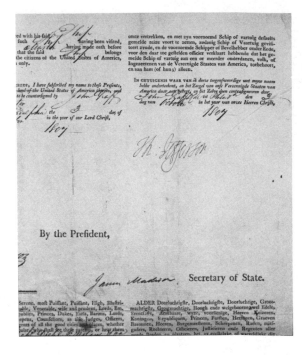

Document signed by *Thomas Jefferson* and *James Madison*. In recent years, documents signed by two men who became president have become highly popular as framed pieces. Value: $3000–$4000.

An Intimate Hobby

In this chapter we have attempted to impart the basic fact that autograph collecting is usually a much more personal endeavor than are most collectibles hobbies. Your own inimitable tastes will frequently dominate your particular collection. Notables you don't like or admire will be relegated to minor investment on your part, but the celebrities of your choice will probably be acquired with what borders on obsession.

Many fans of Greta Garbo, Marilyn Monroe, Elvis Presley, actor James Dean, John Wayne, Sydney "O. Henry" Porter, John Steinbeck, William Faulkner, Albert Einstein, Thomas Edison, George Washington, Abraham Lincoln, Robert E. Lee, Thomas Jefferson, Horatio Nelson, Catherine the Great, Elizabeth the First, Mark Twain, Thomas Wolfe, John F. Kennedy, Lou Gehrig, Babe Ruth, yea, even the redoubtable Button Gwinnett—whose signatures all sell for thousands of dollars—care not what it costs to display something actually signed by an idol, as long as it is guaranteed to be authentic!

As noted dealers and former autograph auctioneers Charles and Diane Hamilton wrote in their 1973 book *Big Name Hunting:* "You don't have to be either wealthy or influential to begin your own collection of autographs.'' It is a challenging hobby, and if you have decided to join those of us already actively involved in it, know that you are embarking on one of the most consistently exciting ventures of your lifetime. Historically important people are about to become some of your best-understood friends and most valuable assets.

Where to Spend Your Money

If you are a serious novice autograph collector, the most important influence upon you and your collection will be the knowledgeable autograph dealer. It is the professional or "career" dealer who will astutely guide you and introduce you to the treasures that you never imagined existed or were available. The sooner you discover the dealer or dealers with whom you are comfortable, the sooner your collection will begin to grow properly and embrace items of importance and value.

Autograph Dealers

There are currently over 100 experienced, responsible, educated, integrity-bound autograph dealers in the United States and overseas. From their voluminous archives you can choose to purchase only the very best of authentic manuscripts, letters, documents, books, and signatures. The majority of full-time dealers publish a monthly or bimonthly catalog which painstakingly itemizes, describes, and prices the most recently available material. Numerous part-time dealers—people with primary income from other interests or careers—also issue catalogs, but these catalogs are often not as regular nor as detailed. In either case, you will find good buys in nearly every catalog that comes your way, and you will become highly dependent on their offerings.

It is not our place to recommend specific dealers to our readers, although as owners of one of the nation's largest and finest collections we have been in constant contact with just about every autograph dealer in the world. We find them to be patient, courteous, thoughtful, and sincerely interested in every facet of this hobby. We avoid those dealers

W. J. Mayo, co-founder of the Mayo Brothers Clinic in Minnesota. Such a piece is rare. Value: $300.

who seem to be more concerned with our checkbook than with what goes into our collection books, and you should do the same.

Naturally, there are dealers who specialize in only limited areas of history or collectibility with their focus and inventory exclusively dedicated to such areas as American Revolutionary War figures, Civil War heroes, U.S. presidents, people in science, classical music and opera stars, or movie stars, depending upon the individual dealer's interests. Hence, once you've determined what it is you wish to collect, you have but to write or telephone such dealers and via their catalogs they will each introduce the choices of material they are currently offering.

A few of the dealers charge a small fee for a copy of a catalog simply to cover the high costs of printing and mailing. The fees tend to discourage the thousands of non-purchasing curiosity seekers who have no intention of buying or collecting. Incidentally,

Charles H. Mayo, co-founder of the Mayo Brothers Clinic. Also rare. Value: $300.

that initial charge is frequently refunded by many dealers when they deduct it from the original purchase price of whatever item you may order. Some of these catalogs are really worth your investment as they are well written and often feature much-needed facsimiles of signatures and handwriting, plus handsome photographs of the more valuable autograph material.

We list alphabetically most of the dealers and auction houses we know and fully respect in *The Price Guide to Autographs.* These are the dealers with longevity, dependability, total honesty, wisdom, and thorough knowledge of autographs with whom we've enjoyed personal buying experiences over the past 30 years.

We shall not, on these pages, point out any one or two dealers for recommendation because that would be terribly unfair to the majority. As you personally become better acquainted with the hobby and the dealers, you will discover that you somehow prefer

The immortal *Clark Gable* was a frequent guest star on Sanders's nationally syndicated interview shows.

Academy Award–winning actor *Gary Cooper* and Sanders chat on the sidelines during a Hollywood charity softball game in the 1950s.

When Sanders was awarded the Radio-TV Personality of the Year title by a national magazine, Academy Award–winning actress *Ginger Rogers* presented him with the silver cup.

Kim Novak

Actress *Kim Novak* was starring in *Vertigo* at Paramount when she was interviewed by George Sanders.

Lee de Forest

Dr. Lee de Forest, father of modern electronics, whose invention of the three-element vacuum tube in 1906 led to the development of radio, long-distance telephony, sound movies, and television. Shown during an interview with Sanders.

Rare glossy 8″ × 10″ signed photograph with the signatures of *Gus Grissom, Edward White,* and *Roger Chaffee*, who died in the first NASA rocket accident. Picture also includes the signature of *James McDivitt.* Value: $1,000.

the attitude, sense of humor, general knowledge, responsiveness, and sincere interest in your particular collection that is offered by one or two dealers. Special personalities or characteristics will draw you to just a few dealers with whom you will become closely associated for many years.

Some of the older dealers are brusque, short-tempered, and impatient with the new collector, and we presume such shortsighted bad manners costs them money and customers they can apparently afford to lose. When they have treated us poorly, we have simply crossed them off our buying list and spent our money with other more patient and understanding souls. We trust you will do likewise.

Part-Time Dealers

In recent times, as this hobby really began to grow, many part-time autograph dealers emerged who are often as enthusiastic, helpful, and friendly as is humanly possible.

However, as in any collectible hobby, many such fledgling dealers have only small inventories and little of the long-term expertise that a seller of autograph material should possess. Such dealers may mean well, but because of their lack of experience in the field they are in many cases poor judges of forgeries and inaccurate about historical facts.

Unfortunately, the hobby's emergence as an excellent investment for surplus capital has drawn some "quick-buck" dealers who are downright dishonest. This type of con artist offers signed photographs they know to be bogus plus flea-market junk that never should surface among serious collectors.

We even know of a few charlatans suspected of actually signing their own supply of forged Hollywood photographs, with the wife falsely signing for the female stars and the husband busily "pen-pretending" to be all of the male stars from Lionel Barrymore to Sabu, the elephant boy! Such nefarious characters are not successful for too long because such fine organizations as the Manuscript Society and the Universal Autograph Collectors Club are vigilant and frequently expose such criminal machinations wherever possible. Likewise, honest competitive dealers are also forever on the lookout for such dishonesty and are quick to report any activities that would be detrimental to this growing hobby.

Once you have discovered the dealer or dealers with whom you intend to work, share your collection hopes and desires forthrightly and they will assist you in building an outstanding, worthwhile autograph collection. Be frank and let them know what kind of budget you have. Don't discuss intentions to buy expensive material that you could never really afford. Sending out such false signals wastes the dealer's valuable time, as well as your own. In other words, why, as Shakespeare wrote, "saw the air" with discussions concerning your "great need" for a General Robert E. Lee handwritten letter (at a cost in excess of $3,000 for a routine missive) when you only have $375 to spend? Your favorite dealer will usually level with you if you have established a good relationship.

Our initial experience with a professional, full-time dealer took place over 30 years ago when we discovered the oldest existing autograph dealership in America, Walter R. Benjamin Autographs Co., Inc., then located on Madison Avenue in New York City. The grande dame of the autograph world, then and now, is Ms. Mary Benjamin, who, with her charming and capable nephew, Christopher C. Jaeckel, runs a major firm with a tradition that covers over 100 years in the autograph business.

Without Ms. Benjamin's canny advice, cautionary thoughts, and sound business practices, our personal interest and ever-increasing investment might never have continued in those early days. With that company in mind, we now mention something extremely important to you and your money. Never, under any circumstances, purchase autograph material "as is," with no guarantee. Every honest dealership guarantees the authenticity of everything it sells, just as the Benjamin organization has done for over a century.

Insist on a Warranty!

A full, prompt, money-back warranty if the piece you purchase has in any way been misrepresented is the custom, not the exception. This is the one hobby, thanks to the efforts of many excellent participating dealers, in which your authentication stands the test of time. If any dealer hesitates to give such a "lifetime" complete money-back guarantee, refrain from buying anything that dealer offers. If a dealer is certain that what he or she has described is truly genuine, why should that dealer be hesitant to offer an ironclad guarantee?

In over three decades, in which we have personally invested hundreds of thousands of dollars for outstanding material, we have never dealt with a dealer who has intentionally attempted to mislead us. The hobby is generally blessed with integrity, especially when one deals with well-established autograph firms.

When Not to Haggle

By the way, don't expect to haggle or "horse-trade" with the better-known dealers, as they are customarily offering extraordinary material that is much in demand. Why should a dealer even consider negotiating a price other than the one indicated in his or her catalog for a rare Thomas Jefferson letter or document? Anyone can sell such Jefferson letters all day long at high, established prices, so why should a dealer spend time dickering with an individual customer over price?

We've had newcomer buyers telephone and literally beg for our Abraham Lincoln pieces, Albert Einstein documents, and Greta Garbo letters, and then attempt to negotiate a lower price than the one we indicated at the outset of the conversation. Such amateurs are quickly informed that we, along with every top dealer or collector in America, have a waiting list of clients who would be delighted to have such rare material at any fair price!

The Rarity Factor

Now we must take a few moments of your reading time to discuss what we like to call "the rarity factor." No dealer and no price guide can ever accurately detail in monetary terms what the rarity factor does to the constantly rising prices of excellent autograph material.

For example, let us imagine that President Abraham Lincoln actually signed a total of 10,000 pieces of paper, including letters to loved ones, official documents as a young

Prominent World War II and NATO leader General *Alfred M. Gruenther* was hosted by Sanders, CEO of a broadcast station in Portland, Oregon.

The signature of *William Henry Harrison,* the U.S. president who served the shortest term in office, has become very popular among autograph collectors because of "the rarity factor." Value: $1,000.

Illinois attorney, Congressional messages, and all of the presidential papers from 1861 to 1865. A good proportion of the above would have been lost or destroyed by fire, flood, silverfish, rust, and general human carelessness. Perhaps 75 percent of such material remains. That might leave approximately 7,500 or more Lincoln pieces available to institutions, the National Archives, private galleries, dealers, and collectors. According to autograph expert Charles Hamilton, in 1978 there were well over 2 million people collecting autographs, with around 20,000 serious collectors out there hunting. Just about every collector wants at least one Lincoln piece in his or her home. Even if our figures are way off the mark, there just are not enough Lincoln autographs to go around!

Hence, the prices on such special material expand yearly, sometimes monthly, because that old devil "the rarity factor" has become a most important consideration. You'll understand the rarity factor much more clearly when you first begin to search for pieces from General George Custer, "Stonewall" Jackson, or Jeb Stuart, or from folks like Kit Carson, Davey Crockett, or actor James Dean. The letters or signed photographs of Greta Garbo are rare, as are signed photographs of Marilyn Monroe and signatures of golfer Bobby Jones, Lou Gehrig, and hundreds of other personalities. You may own some of these one day if you are a determined collector, but you won't ever find them at "bargain basement" prices. They are better than gilt-edged bonds, as the prices on such treasures seldom seem to decrease.

Country and western music stars *Hank Williams, Jr.* and *Merle Kilgore* with emcee Sanders in the 1960s.

Captain George G. Crissman, USN

With Captain *George S. Crissman*, aboard the *U.S.S. Toledo*, George Sanders hosted the first live television program aired from ship to shore in 1951.

HIMALAYAN TRUST

MEDICAL SUB-COMMITTEE:
DR. MAX PEARL.
10 MORVERN ROAD
MT. EDEN
AUCKLAND, 4

CHAIRMAN: SIR EDMUND HILLARY
278A REMUERA ROAD
AUCKLAND
NEW ZEALAND

Sept 2nd, 1980

The Summit of Everest
May 29th 1953

Sir Edmund Hillary had recently conquered Mount Everest when George Sanders had the opportunity to welcome him to the United States.

119

Auctions

More than ever before, prominent and thoroughly reliable auction houses have entered the autograph field with their frequently splendid offerings. Many auction lots are manuscripts or other written material that has been garnered from fine private collections, from institutions raising money for other more important needs, or from dealers who make a profit by auctioning material that did not sell as readily in their catalogs as they might have hoped. Many inheritors of large estates discover such material among the family treasures and, not being interested in autographs, also release it to the auctioneer's hammer.

When previously mentioned New York autograph expert, author, dealer, and auction house owner Charles Hamilton retired, the huge void he left in the auction field was promptly filled by the personable New York schoolteacher, autograph dealer, and former president of the Universal Autograph Collectors Club, Herman Darvick. Darvick's successful auction company specializes in autographs and seldom offers anything else. It will be well worth your time and money to subscribe to Darvick's catalogs, which are always a treasure trove of autographs any collector would love to own.

Other auction "wish books" will come to your from Christie's, Sotheby's, Swann Galleries, Richard C. Frajola, Riba Auctions, Waverly's, Robert G. Kaufmann's, William A. Fox Inc., British newcomer T. Vennett-Smith, Phillips, East Coast, R.M. Smythe, J.A. Stargardt (Marburg, Germany), and many others. We also recommend that you subscribe to some of the auctions that are primarily concerned with the sale of philatelic or stamp collections. They frequently offer free-frank covers and other related autographed envelopes, letters, and documents laden with tax revenue stamps. Sometimes a bargain can be obtained among all that precious collectible postage.

Here we must add another note of caution to the new collector. Though the major auction houses make every reasonable effort to offer only genuine material, there have been many instances when their employees have mistakenly described an auction lot to be something it was not. It is always your job to study both the catalog description and the item itself when it is delivered to your home or office. Don't assume anything! You must check your material promptly and carefully once it is in your hands as you are allowed only a brief grace period during which you can return faulty material to the auction house. The auction house will refund your money, but you must read the instructions in every catalog regarding the time allowed to return something that is either bogus or was improperly represented. If you miss the deadline, you will probably be terribly unhappy and disappointed, not to mention without your investment.

Some of these hazards can be avoided. If you can afford to do it, pay a small commission and have one of the professional dealers or agents, who always attend public autograph auctions, inspect the material you wish to buy *prior* to the auction during the allotted preview hours and then later bid for you from the floor. That way your agent has actually studied the material you want and is certain that you will be satisfied. Obviously, if you have the time, attend the auctions yourself and enjoy the indescribable thrill of having your bid top all others as you pray the auctioneer's gavel will rap on his desk once you've offered the highest bid you intend to make on the lot of your dreams.

Galleries and Other Posh Sources

As you may have noticed, many beautifully framed autograph items are currently being presented at over a hundred posh autograph galleries located in spacious malls, chic shopping areas, and exclusive department stores throughout the United States. In these luxurious settings you will find some of the world's rarest and most expensive autographic collectibles.

As you stroll through such galleries, your heart will begin to flutter as you gaze longingly upon museum-framed documents, letters, photographs, etc., all meticulously matted, highlighted with brass or engraved nameplates, artistically illuminated, and bearing what we call "Tiffany" price tags.

Because of the recent upsurge of international interest in specially framed autographed artifacts among former collectors of prints, lithographs, and oil or watercolor artworks, the aforementioned galleries are prospering. Once you've seen the splendor of creative framing in a comfortable gallery setting, you will probably understand why the galleries charge very high prices. Because of a gallery's obviously costly overhead caused by horrendous rents for such valuable sales space, its need to be staffed with properly informed sales people, advertising, and the cost of acquiring and maintaining a large and valuable inventory, the gallery owner must demand higher prices if he or she intends to remain in business.

As always, it will be your personal, considered decision as to your preference in shopping for autographs. If you are simply shopping for a very special single autograph treasure to adorn the walls of your lovely home or apartment, you will be well served by such galleries despite their high fees. The galleries have added a glorious new dimension to this already unusual hobby.

Morality in Dealing

Once you have begun to feel secure in your personal judgments as a collector, there will be opportunities for you to purchase material from the proverbial little old lady or man who is cleaning out the attic or basement only to discover a trove of signed goodies. If you treat these uninformed souls as considerately as *you* would like to be treated by a more knowledgeable buyer, your collection will grow without diminishing your morality. It really doesn't cost very much more to be fair and aboveboard with prospective amateur sellers. If you show them what the current market indicates is a fair price and carefully explain what their alternatives are, you'll probably find, as we have, that they will be delighted to cooperate. You will have the coveted autographs, and they will have the unexpected cash.

The amateur sellers you have treated fairly will report your ''wonderfulness'' to friends, relatives, and neighbors, who will soon be calling you to ask if you'd be interested in the great presidential document an uncle left to them years ago. Honesty, like magic, creates surprisingly spectacular results for the decent collector.

Bookstores: Sources of Treasure

Don't forget to rummage through the dusty bookshelves in your neighborhood store that sells old books. There you will find autographed books signed by your favorite authors at reasonable prices. You might even get lucky, as we have, and discover John Hancock signatures, or a Thomas Jefferson document, carefully placed between the pages of an antiquated book that the bookseller had somehow overlooked.

Many of our very best buys are found in the old bookstores located all over this country. The back roads can lead to very fine autographic discoveries. We find that numerous antique dealers have ancient paper stored in a back room or under the counter just waiting for you to stop by and make a legitimate offer.

It has become increasingly difficult to locate naïve sellers of rare material. Most people know what the average prices ought to be and are not standing by awaiting the opportunity to be fleeced.

It's a saner, safer market now, one in which you can invest with some sense of security. The more you study this hobby, the better and wiser your investment. In this volume we have listed books by other authors that we feel will not only add to your knowledge of autographs but will make you a much better collector. You are embarking on a most memorable treasure hunt that should bring you great pride of ownership, and we wish you an autographic bon voyage.

How to Reach the Stars

Since the challenging hobby of autograph collecting began several centuries ago, collectors have been devising ingenious methods of acquiring the precious signatures, letters, manuscripts, and documents of the world's most famous and infamous celebrities. Gaining in-person access to some rather elusive, intentionally difficult luminaries who often are professionally shielded from the general public is one of the most difficult and frustrating aspects of this avocation.

In-Person Autographs

Obviously, the most instantly rewarding autograph-collecting procedure is to be where your idol is going to be and to join the other autograph-seekers with their pens in hand and their autograph books, index cards, or photographs ready to be politely offered to the celebrated one so that he or she can quickly sign *in person!* Autograph collectors know that the stars appear in public places to entertain. Such stars perform in concert halls, auditoriums, sports arenas, hotel or casino dining rooms, and theaters of every size in every large community in the world, as well as in radio and television studios, motion picture sound stages, and even at spacious convention centers.

There are literally thousands of opportunities for the aspiring collector personally to request a celebrity's autograph. Most of the celebrities respond graciously and thoughtfully to the eager collectors who crowd around them at nearly every public appearance.

Some in-person autograph collectors are almost uncanny in uncovering the public whereabouts of the stars. They locate them when the celebrities are on vacation, dining out, on buying sprees in exclusive shops and malls, honeymooning, visiting friends, or attending movie premieres or other star-studded shows.

If you are to participate in assembling such in-person signature acquisitions, you had best begin to study local newspapers and watch your hometown television news or gossip programs to become aware of the comings and goings of such celebrities in your own community. Famous people are usually not static—their careers keep them forever on the move. Every sizable town in America is visited, at one time or another, by the rich, the famous, the successful, the political, the learned, the sought-after. Prepare yourself for the possibility of contacting some special person right in your hometown by being constantly alert and vigilant as you make yourself aware of their potential visits to your area.

A Little Creativity

One clever collector of our wide acquaintance discovered an ingenious method to gain spectacular in-person signatures where the stars couldn't ever refuse him or escape his proffered autograph book. When this U.S. millionaire collector retired from a lengthy broadcasting career in 1977, like so many comfortable retirees he realized that suddenly he had a considerable amount of spare time on his hands. Having been a highly successful executive in both radio and television, he knew exactly where to go to add to his already huge autograph collection without his friends discovering his eccentric, novel, and temporary career. He patiently watched the newspapers until he spied the help-wanted advertisement in the *Los Angeles Times* he'd been waiting to see. Our autograph hound applied for and was hired as a security guard at the NBC studios in Burbank, California.

Within a week, resplendent in his dark blue uniform complete with brass badge and Sam Browne leather belt, plus the ever-present dark sunglasses, he was stationed at the main guard gate. Celebrities who appeared at NBC on "The Tonight Show," news programs, or other nighttime guest appearances from December 15, 1977, to February 15, 1978, were stopped by our amateur guard and, while seated in their vehicles, barred by an automatic electric gate, which he controlled from the small guardhouse. The celebrities were then politely requested to sign his thick, leather-bound autograph book.

Assuming this was some new NBC security regulation to be strictly obeyed before gaining entrance to the studio, each and every star signed without the slightest hesitation. In just 60 days this short-term guard collected the signatures of over 250 stars, including 35 Academy Award winners (such as James Stewart, Anne Baxter, Jack Lemmon, Anthony Quinn, Bette Davis, Burt Lancaster, John Wayne, and Ingrid Bergman), big-name rock-and-roll stars (such as Ringo Starr and Bruce Springsteen), sports stars, political leaders (including a former actor named Ronald Reagan), and many other hard-to-meet people-in-the-news.

A few years later, he sold the albums he had filled at the NBC gate for several

Best Regards

Ronald Reagan

5/27/65

Nancy and *Ronald Reagan* were regulars on radio and television programs hosted by Sanders in the 1950s.

thousand dollars, making him the highest-paid short-term security guard who ever lived! Incidentally, our highly creative gate guard's career was shortened when "The Tonight Show" host, Johnny Carson, complained to NBC authorities that his Mercedes coupe had been stopped at the entrance twice and that he had been literally "forced" to sign an "entry book" before being permitted to enter the main gate. On one of Carson's forced stops, he muttered to the creative guard, "What the hell do you do, pull out a gun and shoot 'em if they don't stop and sign?" Johnny's complaint was well-timed, however, as our retiree was planning on leaving his post for a lengthy vacation in the Greek islands.

More Creativity

Speaking of "creative" autograph collecting, we are truly impressed with the research and all-out effort of autograph dealer Jerry Granat of Hewlett, New York. Granat initiated a very lengthy written correspondence with Adolf Hitler's infamous architect, Albert Speer.

Following months of highly provocative questioning by Granat, Speer agreed to meet with him in Europe. Within a few weeks, Ellen and Jerry Granat were dining with this one-time Nazi leader in Munich. He answered most of their questions regarding his knowledge, or lack of it, regarding the Holocaust, World War II, and his participation in Hitler's hierarchy. Needless to say, the Granat's own a fabulous collection of Albert Speer's writings. They enjoyed a fantastic personal experience because of the exciting hobby of autograph collecting! Ironically, Granat was able to convince Speer to contribute $1,000 to the United Jewish Appeal.

The Best Places to Obtain In-Person Autographs

In 1981, autograph dealer-auctioneer Herman Darvick wrote that "the best cities for collecting autographs in person are New York, Los Angeles, and Washington, D.C." To that list we would now add San Francisco, Atlanta, Miami, Seattle, Phoenix, and all other large cities that have developed huge convention complexes. Internationally, we believe that London, Geneva, Rome, Paris, and the French Riviera offer the most famous in-person faces.

Autograph dealer and Washington, D.C. attorney Edward N. Bomsey should be included in the "creative acquirer" category. For many years he has faithfully served the Republican Inaugural Committee with the planning and presentation of the gala inaugural festivities every four years since President Jimmy Carter's departure from the Washington scene. Bomsey is usually rewarded with in-person signings of his and his wife's inaugural programs by the incoming President and Vice President. His special energy and knowledge has helped him glean some of America's most precious signatures and inscriptions, actually penned in his presence. Signatures can't be more authentic than those!

The Right Equipment

If you do decide to become an in-person autograph collector, be certain to carry the necessary equipment. You should always have a small supply of 3 × 5 cards or a compact autograph book, plus several working pens. To paraphrase the famous credit card company's advertisement: "Don't leave home without them." You never know when someone famous or worthwhile, preferably both, will cross your particular path.

Always, without exception, request the autograph you seek in your most courteous tones and with the best of manners. Don't tug at the celebrity's clothes, don't push or shove, and don't ever assume that a signature on a piece of paper or on the pages of your book is something the celebrity owes you.

Willingness to Sign

It is our experience that if you are exceedingly polite, the celebrity responds in kind and is frequently grateful for your attention. There will be a few exceptions, such as the boorish Sean Penn, the haughty Joanne Woodward, or the totally inaccessible Greta Garbo—who frequently rewarded autograph seekers with a healthy clout to the side of the head with her hefty handbag when she walked on Manhattan sidewalks.

Until recent years, the late Miss Garbo was not only amazingly evasive but also handled that always-present handbag with all the athletic prowess of Steffi Graf. It has been documented by the walking wounded that Garbo's forehand with said handbag sent several collectors sprawling, ducking, and fleeing whenever they blocked her passage.

Actor Paul Newman was certainly justified in finally deciding that the rudeness of unthinking autograph hounds was too much for him to bear. As the Academy Award–winning actor tells it: "I was standing at a urinal in a public restroom, and this guy next to me sticks a pen and index card in my face and asks for my autograph! I didn't know which hand to use." That witless request and breach of courtesy was the contributing factor in causing Newman, who is really a very nice guy, to determine never to sign in public again, a vow he has kept religiously for many years. Likewise, over the years Marlon

Actor *Paul Newman* and Sanders share some "moonshine" on the set of "The Helen Morgan Story" at Warner Bros. in the 1950s. This was before Newman stopped giving autographs.

Brando, Frank Sinatra, and Cary Grant have revealed in personal interviews that it was the rude behavior of some "autograph pests" that made them finally say, "No autographs, ever!"

Autograph-seekers must understand that because of terrorists, thieves, kooks, and even cold-blooded assassins, many celebrated people are carefully protected by a phalanx of security guards or secret service people. These specially trained security forces are paid handsomely to surround and obscure from public view those who employ them, generally warding off any potential dangers of human contact.

You will discover that few of these large professional escorts will relent and permit any autograph-seekers to knife through the crowd and reach the star. Can we blame them for such tight security measures considering the assassinations, in such crowds, of Robert F. Kennedy and John Lennon, as well as the attempts on the lives of President Ronald Reagan, President Gerald Ford, and Governor George Wallace of Alabama? Without exception, all of the personalities just mentioned were once delighted to sign autographs while strolling through crowds in public places.

Dangerous times and mean streets have changed the availability to the collector of such people. When little-known Hollywood actresses are murdered or maimed by psychopaths you can expect security to tighten around all of your favorite personalities. It is a pity, but your chances of persuading a Secret Service agent that the President of the United States should sign your book or photograph is asking for a special privilege that could cost the agent his or her job for negligence in the performance of security duties. Only those people wearing proper official badges of identification can ever convince the Secret Service to relax the rules just a little bit. Until America's streets are safe once again, it is better to forgo the autograph today, lest a life be lost tomorrow with lazy, flawed, or careless security.

Obtaining Autographs by Mail

Despite what has been said above, it is best to acquire all such autographs in person, when possible, because of their obvious authenticity. However, countless collectors remind us that they happen to live in remote areas of America and find it much easier to write clever letters requesting autograph material. Such activity has become a cottage industry for many dealers who frequently disguise themselves to the signer as being small-time collectors.

In any case, thousands of collectors from all over the world dutifully mail out their photographs, programs, index cards, album leaves, typescripts, first-day covers, sketches, baseballs, and other memorabilia to be signed. Hundreds of celebrities agree to sign and then return the various postage-paid envelopes or packages to the respective collectors.

It is wise to spend considerable time composing a unique but brief form letter that can be sent to the people you are hoping will return your precious material. Some of the earlier how-to books on collecting autographs offered examples of simple requests and the forms that such missives should take. Unfortunately, there are now millions of collectors mailing out such trite little messages, and the stars and their secretaries weary of receiving them.

You must be creative and thoughtful. Think of new ways to attract the stars' attention and make them really want to cooperate with you and be delighted to add their pen scratchings to your particular collection.

An excellent example of such fertile thinking came from former high school teacher and now full-time autograph dealer Charles Searle of Woodbine, Georgia. He and his wife Pat came up with the idea of asking famous people to sign both their stage or pen names *and* their real names. Much to the Searle's surprise, about 60 or 70 different stars were delighted to sign both of their names in full.

Searle had similar success when he requested that various actors, authors, artists, and other celebrities simply draw a self-caricature or a doodle. He was amazed with the results and the artistic ingenuity of the personalities to whom he wrote. In fact, nearly 500 responded, thereby creating an autograph collection of tremendous value.

An Artful Method of Obtaining Autographs

It goes without saying that some autograph collectors who amass collections by mail are more talented than others. For example, Canadian artist Jack Ellison, who is employed

Canadian artist Jack Ellison has created a special style with his colorful sketches of contemporary greats. This *Joe DiMaggio* original sells for $100.

Another superb example of Canadian artist Jack Ellison's artwork. This signed *Willy Mays* drawing is priced at $100.

Artist Jack Rosen's colorful signed caricatures of the rich and the famous have become popular collector's items. This *Ernest Hemingway* is one of Rosen's best. Value: $1,000.

M. H. Herrin, an artist who drew some covers for *Time* magazine, asked celebrities to sign his original sketches. *Edward VIII* signed this sketch while king. Value: $1,000.

An original M. H. Herrin sketch signed by Sweden's *King Gustav V.* Value: $1,000.

by a large Toronto ad agency, draws an original portrait of each personality whose autograph he seeks. Using a secret technique, he draws the sketch from a favorite photograph of the celebrity and then mails the original Ellison sketch with the request that it be autographed and returned to him. A copy of the original sketch is given to the celebrity for his or her own personal collection of memorabilia. Because the stars receive a stunning drawing of one of their own favorite poses, they have been extremely responsive. Hence, artist Ellison enjoys an 80 percent success ratio in recovering his signed artwork.

Ellison is not the first professional artist to use such a ploy. New York cartoonist Jack Rosen and the brilliant artist M. H. Herrin, whose magnificent pencil portraits of the world's most powerful and famous people graced *Time* magazine's covers for many years, also sent original sketches to be autographed and made a copy for each signer to keep.

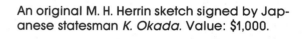

An original M. H. Herrin sketch signed by Japanese statesman *K. Okada.* Value: $1,000.

An original M. H. Herrin sketch signed by South Africa's soldier-statesman General *Jan Christiaan Smuts.* Value: $1,000.

Lip print and signature of Academy Award—winning actress *Angelica Huston.*

Lip print and signature of actress *Lee Remick.*

Persistence and Creativity Pay

Another collector-dealer of our acquaintance, Charles "Chuck" McKeen, has mailed out as many as 500 pieces to be signed per day, thanks to the marvels of the computer. In the past seven years, McKeen has spent over $7,000 per year in postage alone. However, his mail return of autographs of sports stars, film and stage personalities, and general people-in-the-news types is staggeringly huge, and his sales profits from other dealers, who buy his extra copies, has given him a handsome profit for years without his leaving home. Most of today's professional autograph dealers began their careers with just such mailings. Why not you?

McKeen has come up with other novel notions. He asked glamorous movie stars to place their lip prints on 3 × 5 index cards and then add their signatures. He was amazed at how many "mailed" kisses he received. We have reproduced a few examples in the accompanying illustrations.

Chuck also had sports stars outline with a pen or pencil their hands on paper or heavy cardboard and then signed beneath the hand print. The jocks thought it was such

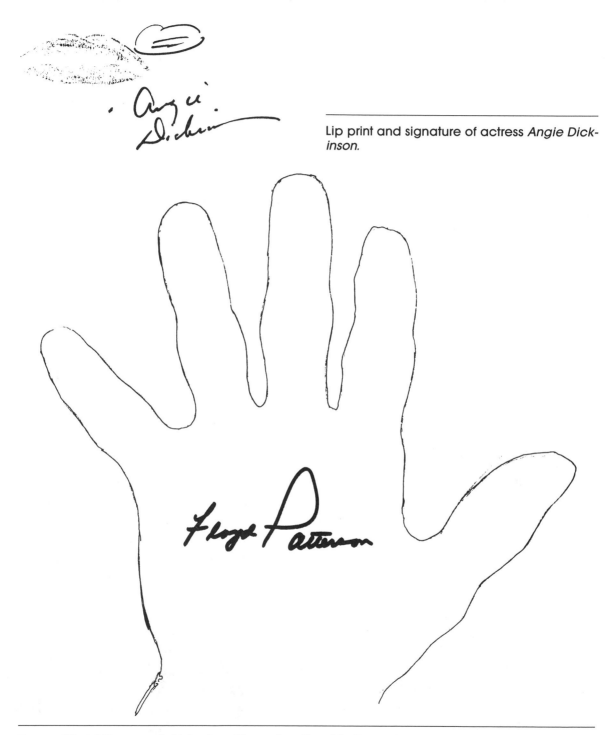

Lip print and signature of actress *Angie Dickinson.*

Former World Heavyweight Boxing Champion *Floyd Patterson* hand outline and signature.

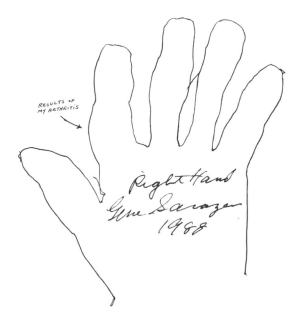

RESULTS OF
MY ARTHRITIS

Right Hand
Gene Sarazen
1988

Golf's legendary *Gene Sarazen* outlined his hand and then autographed the drawing for Sanders.

a great idea that not only did many cooperate but they also congratulated McKeen for his innovation. Hall of Fame Golfer Gene Sarazen even drew arrows to various points of his hands where swellings indicated severe arthritis.

But Don't Get Too Creative

Sometimes "creative thinking" gets out of control with unfortunate results. Let us tell you about the nefarious Philadelphia collector who wrote a most untruthful message to many foreign heads of state proclaiming the birth of his firstborn son whom he was purportedly naming after the regal or republican heads to whom he wrote.

All went well for years as this scheming character received beautiful signed photographs from various presidents, monarchs, prime ministers, sultans, and other assorted world leaders. Each of the heads of state apparently believed that this magical child bore his or her first and sometimes second name.

Then there was a special United Nations gathering of dignitaries in New York City a few years ago. The cunning letter writer and his neighbors were astonished to find a huge motorcade complete with accompanying security guards and the ever-present press corps all marching up to his front door. With the bright TV lights focused on his entrance, the suitably embarrassed autograph collector timidly opened his door.

Much to his surprise, there stood the toothy, unshaven leader of the PLO, who had come to visit little "Yasir Arafat, Jr.!" Of course, the "babe," now age 15, had never been given such a name, and everyone involved felt more than mildly sheepish. The real Yasir pushed his way back to the limousine at curbside muttering Arabic invectives directed at "ze phony infidels." The man from the Middle East who wears the checkered towel around his usually unkempt head has never returned to Philadelphia and may never again believe another letter-writer from America who is seeking an autograph.

Actually, it is not necessary to be dishonest in requesting material from world leaders. There are many whose secretaries will see to it that your letter is seriously considered and frequently replied to with a signature on an official card created for just such requests. Sometimes the collector is even blessed with a polite signed letter accompanying a formal and handsomely autographed photograph. The exception is requests sent to the British Royal Family, whose secretarial minions will reply by formal mail that "their Royal Majesties simply do not communicate or autograph anything for anyone with whom they are not personally acquainted."

Finding Addresses

Some readers may wonder how one acquires correct addresses of famous people. Most celebrities do not wish to have their home addresses published for obvious reasons, but you can still find those addresses.

The very best source is available in most public libraries. It is titled *Who's Who in America* (45th edition, 1987–1988, published by Marquis). Following each person's brief biography in this book you will find listed a business and a home address. Most celebrities, by the way, prefer that you address your requests to their offices if they have them.

This three-volume collection of famous Americans carries thousands of correct names and addresses that should keep your typewriter active for some time. As we have indicated previously, it is your responsibility as the autograph-seeker to include all return postage whenever you forward material to be signed. Enclose a self-addressed and stamped envelope that is large enough to transport properly the signed piece or pieces back to your home or office.

Various dealers in "the addresses of the stars" have amassed huge address lists which they sell to new collectors. If that approach appeals to you then you will discover that there are many sources. Two of note are ACS of Los Angeles, whose star addresses are always current, and Celebrity Addresses, available from Karen and Roger Christensen of San Diego, California. However, our personal experience with most Hollywood stars tells us that most of the contemporary addresses route your requests to the offices of press agents, personal managers, studio public relations directors, and secretaries, plus

Comedian *Bob Hope* was a frequent guest on radio and television shows hosted by George and Helen Sanders. Here Bob and George chat at Bob's Toluca Lake home in 1955.

Susan Hayward

Redheaded *Susan Hayward* had just received her 1958 Best Actress of the Year Oscar; here, she describes her reaction to television host Sanders.

Long before he played Ben Matlock, his most recent television incarnation, *Andy Griffith* was a frequent guest on Sanders's syndicated programs in Hollywood.

William Holden

Academy Award-winning actor *William Holden* was a longtime friend of Sanders, seen here at a Hollywood party.

cadres of hangers-on who are flagrantly permitted to serve as signers of thousands of various-sized photographs and cards. There are literally scores of glossy black-and-white or color photographs being represented as having been signed in person when actually the star signs practically nothing and leaves the tiring chore to underpaid underlings.

As an example, when Michael J. Fox of "Family Ties" fame was receiving thousands of pieces of mail per day at his studio, he had very little time available to peruse such correspondence or to reply personally to any of it. Think about it. He was receiving more daily mail than the president of the United States!

Fox worked on his popular TV series from dawn to dusk, six days a week, and had to memorize his lines when he was at home. Add to that some small semblance of a personal life plus necessary public appearances—now when does the naïve autograph collector imagine that Fox could find time to communicate personally with the millions of fans who have purchased a home address that is supposedly accepting tons of his mail daily? Likewise, the average member of Congress in Washington, D.C., receives approximately 5,000 pieces of mail each month. That's why there are more Autopens in our nation's capital than anywhere else in the world.

Beware of Publicity Departments

When two of the three authors of this book worked in Hollywood, from 1945 to 1960, we spent considerable time cooperating with the publicity departments at MGM, 20th Century Fox, Columbia, RKO, and Warner Brothers, as well as at Paramount, where one of our business partners in a nationally syndicated radio show was also a studio departmental head.

During that time at Paramount, we regularly saw, in person, a paid staff of female secretaries "forging" signatures on the attractive 8" × 10" glossy publicity photos of Marlon Brando, Ingrid Bergman, Charlton Heston, Bing Crosby, and many, many others. This we saw with our own eyes! It has been an established Hollywood practice since the 1920s. Yet, we still have uninformed peddlers of such worthless trash attempting to convince us that such material is collectible. In reality, it is valuable only as Hollywood memorabilia because the forged or "secretarial" signatures are worthless oddities. Hence, as in all things purchasable, "let the buyer beware!"

The Thrill of the Hunt

Knowledge is the key to any hobby. And while they are rare, there are big finds to be made in autograph collecting, and the thrill will last you a lifetime—*if you recognize that rare treasure when you stumble across it!*

Helen Sanders is one of the lucky ones (and "luck" comes more from knowledge and determination than from four-leaf clovers). Here, in her own words, is how she bagged one of the biggest finds in recent autograph history.

It was just another freezing mid-winter day in the mountains of North Carolina. No snow, but the kind of day that makes you appreciate staying in, with your feet shoved into a pair of sheepskin-lined slippers and with an old out-at-the-elbows sweater wrapped around your torso. Besides that, my husband, George, was suffering from the tail end of bronchitis. He hates the cold. Winter weather bothers him and if there is anything he can blame on it, he will. Most especially, his disposition suffers with the cold.

The point is, he did not want to go out. But the advertising flyer for the auction read "Preview, Friday, 3 to 6 P.M." It also said this was a sale of the effects of a Broadway producer, director, and publicity agent; that there were signed photos of celebrities and a reference to Greta Garbo. That, of course, was the magic word: *Garbo.*

To a collector of autographs, manuscripts, documents, signed photos, and the like, that was, indeed, a magic word. At the time we had some 20,000 pieces, including U.S. presidents, kings, queens, heads of state, scientists, Civil War heroes, musicians, artists, composers, but only one Greta Garbo signature— and most collectors have none. Who knows? I thought. Let's give it a go.

We bundled into our New Zealand sheepskin-lined coats, I braved the elements to pre-warm the car (that was to improve George's temperament), and off we went on another adventure. There are all kinds of treasure hunts, you know. They are not necessarily all for gold, but those that are not can certainly be as lucrative. However, a treasure hunt for gold requires maps and scientific paraphernalia and financial backing—not to mention the *un*mentionable discomfort of the search itself. We, on the other hand, had only to drive to the other side of town, use our God-given brains and eyesight, and make a decision as to whether there was anything of value worth acquiring.

I guess that is an oversimplification of the situation. Most sales of this nature have a preponderance of "things": furniture, lamps, linens, dishes, knickknacks, and the like. But this sale was different in that it was top-heavy with *other* "things": books, signed and unsigned photographs, proofs of unpublished photos, magazines, music, and boxes and boxes and boxes of paper junk.

After saying hello to a few familiar faces, we separated. Each taking a different section of the room we wandered around like a couple of mad "lookie-loos." That was not the way to attack the problem.

"George," I said, "you look at the stand-up material and I'll probe the stuff on the floor."

Fortunately, I was wearing my usual jeans attire and did not mind crawling around to inspect the boxes. The boxes were dirty. The contents of the boxes were dirty. The floor was dirty. The floor was also cold.

Meanwhile, bent over the tables above me, George was investigating the boxes of framed photos. Academy Award winners Helen Hayes, Alice Brady, and Thomas Mitchell, as well as Leslie Howard, Constance Bennett, and Gertrude Lawrence, were among the famous names who had given personally inscribed and signed portraits to the gentleman whose estate was being disbursed. On other tables were large studio portraits and proofs of Greta Garbo. They were not signed, but there were literally hundreds of them separated into lots of about 20 or so.

In my territory on the floor I was discovering 1930s movie magazines with Garbo on the cover, sheet music picturing Garbo and John Gilbert, a box of out-of-print biographies of Garbo, scripts, press releases, newspaper clippings, playbills, and so on. Many of the cardboard cartons were outsize—the size in which paper towels, toilet paper, and tissues are shipped. There were smaller ones, too, all filled to the top with correspondence. Thousands and thousands of pieces. Old bank statements, deeds, utility statements, insurance bills, tax receipts, and letters. They all smelled of mold. Some pieces were damp-stained and bore the remnants of a barrage of silverfish. It really did not look too promising.

Certainly time was of the essence and not adequate enough to explore all those boxes laden with all that correspondence. In leafing through an old scrapbook, however, I discovered a faintly familiar newspaper clipping from a New York daily. It was a photo that I had seen many years before, and it was such a scoop at the time that it had been reprinted many times since in such publications as *Life* magazine.

The candid shot was of Miss Garbo seated at a booth having lunch with a friend. The always camera-shy lady holding her floppy hat over her face to prevent the camera from invading her privacy did not realize that the mirrors to the side and back of her gave a perfect reflection of her unmistakable face. Her luncheon companion was this very same gentleman whose estate was now being fractured.

Fact: He did know her. Therefore, in all these thousands of pieces of paper, there must be at least one piece of paper from Greta Garbo. A cursory examination of one box turned up a letter of famous writer O. O. McIntyre and a telegram from columnist Walter Winchell. Another box held a red-penned "Fannie" from author Fannie Hurst. But most of the mail seemed to be from the gentleman to his mother and from his mother to him. Their letters to each other were five and six pages long—hers, closely handwritten, and his, single-spaced typewritten. As fate would have it, one of the first of his mother's letters I had hurriedly opened had a reference to Garbo in it. Something like, "When is she coming?"

Digging deeper I opened one that seemed never to have been opened because the dampness had resealed the envelope. Another reference: "Thank you again for sharing Greta's letter with me. I will be sure and return any others that you care to send."

There had to be at least *one* pony in there. Somewhere, in all these hundreds of pounds of paper, was a prize! But what I now saw in front of me was an impossible task and certainly the end to an impossible dream. But always the optimist, I knew there had to be a way!

It was just as cold the following morning but I had a sort of lightness of heart and a tremendous exhilaration as I again pre-warmed the car for George. He did not seem quite as irritable. He had taken down the lot numbers of the things he was interested in buying, and I had done likewise. We had arrived early enough to do some more exploring, and the sale was starting just as I crawled out from under a table and joined George at the seats we had marked for ourselves shortly after arriving.

"Find anything interesting?" George asked.

"No, only what I saw yesterday. But there just *has* to be something in there. How about you?"

"All I really want," he answered, "are the two Leslie Howards—and maybe a couple of other things."

The auction was well under way, with several lots of furniture and bric-a-brac going to the highest bidders. Hours went by, and George acquired the two signed, inscribed portraits of the famous British actor, while I waited patiently for the boxes of junk about which I was so optimistic. George, however, is not noted for his patience. He was tired, hungry, coughing, and cold.

Unfortunately, that particular auction room is not known for its efficient heating system. The auction itself? Highly efficient, selling the more important pieces before hunger set in, before the bidders were tired, and before the crowd began to thin out. Of course that meant that my precious boxes might not be sold until the following day.

"Let's go!" George said.

"What about my boxes?"

"To hell with the boxes!"

"But there's got to be Garbo material in them!" (Obviously he did not see the big picture.)

"How many do you want?" he asked with resignation.

"All of them." (I saw the big picture.)

"You're crazy!"

Crazy or not, I wanted them all, and because George wanted to get home he asked the auctioneer to put up the boxes for bids right away. The man was very accommodating and did just that. There was not much enthusiasm—just a couple of bids against us. Another box was put up with the announcement that the highest bidder could have his choice of the balance of the boxes at the same price. Again, we won the bid, and we elected to take the rest of the boxes.

I was happy. George was mad. Those dirty boxes with all those silverfish were *not* coming inside the house, I was informed.

As we trudged back and forth carrying our booty out to the car we became the brunt of some local humor laid on us by the "regulars" who invariably hang together by the exit door. They enjoyed our struggle and wanted to know if we really thought we were going to find something in all that junk. Lifting up a handful of paper and letting it filter through my hands back down into the box I said, "Whatcha sees is whatcha gets."

You may well wonder why the fuss? Why the excitement? Well, in a sense, those boxes represent a giant sweepstakes. Consider each piece of paper as an entry ticket. The prize is a name scribbled on one of those entry tickets—a silly name that isn't even real: *Greta Garbo*. Like any sweepstakes drawing, however, the odds are overwhelmingly against you, but the reward is well worth the effort.

Just think! According to the internationally known autograph expert, Charles Hamilton, a letter written and signed by Greta Garbo is worth more than a letter written and signed by Abraham Lincoln. In fact, a mere signature of the lady was recently sold at a New York auction for almost $1,000. Her autograph is *that* rare. Garbo is absolutely unapproachable and will sign nothing. So this was to be a real live treasure hunt right here in my own home.

I cannot describe my feeling of expectation as I dove into that first box or my feeling of disappointment when I did not find a treasure. However, I really did not know exactly what we were looking for. Everything was in envelopes, so everything had to be opened, taken out, and read. Every canceled check had to be looked at, each endorsement verified.

George helped me, but because he was not feeling well he soon grew tired—not to mention bored. Letters from "Mother" went unopened and into the discard pile along with those from old girl friends. I, too, grew tired of opening letters from the same people, with identical postmarks and written in repeated recognizable handwriting. These, also, joined the discard pile. Please remember, we are talking about thousands of pieces of mail collected over a period of about 80 years. Apparently nothing had ever been thrown away.

The hours passed. George had long since gone to sleep, and there was not a whole lot to show for my efforts. Yes, there were some letters from famous actresses of movies and stage; Zazu Pitts, more from author Fannie Hurst, and an astrological profile of leading lady Gertrude Lawrence. There were theatrical contracts for shows such as "Ramshackle Inn" and "The Two Mrs. Carrolls" with statements showing the daily and weekly receipts of these stage productions, the expenses, salaries, etc. But there was no Garbo letter.

A letter from Kaj Gynt discussed Miss Garbo at great length with suggestions regarding a meeting and the possibility of her playing a part. Then there was the letter I had come across earlier asking, "When is she coming?" *My* interest, of course, was when was *I* going to find something from "The Lady," as she was referred to in the Kaj Gynt communication.

There were love letters from international stage star Eugenie Leontovich, telegrams from British film star Wendy Barrie, invitations from wealthy New York socialite Betty Henderson, and reams of memos on a variety of subjects. One such memo read: "Sept. 18th—G's birthday—Flowers." Now that was promising.

Toward the bottom of the box I was examining I picked up a small envelope. It was addressed by typewriter to the gentleman whose papers we had purchased. It bore a New York City postmark. The back flap was engraved in blue and said "The Hampshire House." It was a short, typed letter, but at the bottom of the page it was signed "GG."

As I looked at the unmistakable initials I let out a yell that not only woke up George but our two doberman pinschers as well. It was after 3:00 A.M. when I finally calmed down enough to go to sleep, but I went with the happy thought that having found *one,* I knew now that there had to be others. Now there was proof that G.G. had actually communicated via the U.S. Post Office.

I began the morning with a very positive attitude, but there was no way to systematize the search because there was no order to the contents. It was a matter of look and learn. So the hunt went on, revealing letters from Elizabeth Bergner, a contract signed by Berthold Brecht, a diary, newspaper clippings linking Garbo to our gentleman, telegrams from Garbo, and a group of letters postmarked Santa Monica and Beverly Hills.

The address on the first of these letters was hand-printed in huge childish letters that covered the entire face of the envelope. The contents were written in pencil on yellow, lined paper, and the writer was thanking the recipient for advice, seeking other advice, and making plans for visiting him in New York. The letter was about three pages in length and signed "HB." I folded it, returned it to its envelope, and tossed it into the discard box. The next similarly addressed piece was a bit longer but unsigned. It joined its mate, and as I ran across more, I treated them in a similar manner, tossing them, unopened, on the pile.

So it went. More bank statements, bills, mother's letters, girl friends' letters, etc., etc., etc. Tired and frustrated, I decided it was time for a break from this seemingly unending job. A book can be relaxing, so I picked up one of the Garbo biographies we had bought at the auction and headed for the most comfortable spot I could find.

I wasn't really concentrating, just sort of scanning the book, skipping from chapter to chapter, but as I flipped through the pages a group of names stood out at the top of one of the pages. Karen Lind and Harriett Brown were among them—names that Greta Garbo uses to maintain her own peculiar brand of privacy. *Harriett Brown?* Of course! "*HB*"!!

A burst of adrenalin shot through me as I raced back to the box where I had discarded all those letters postmarked Santa Monica and Beverly Hills and printed in that large, childish hand. I charged

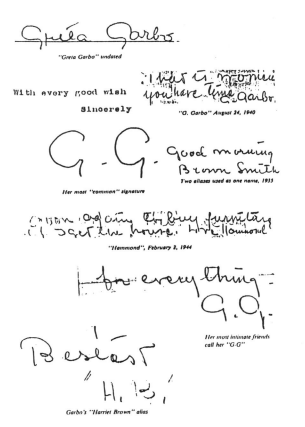

"Greta Garbo" undated

With every good wish

Sincerely

"G. Garbo" August 24, 1940

Her most "common" signature

Two aliases used as one name, 1935

"Hammond", February 2, 1944

Her most intimate friends call her "G-G"

Garbo's "Harriet Brown" alias

Thanks to Helen Sanders's amazing discovery of *Greta Garbo* letters in a box of paper trash at a local auction, here are some excellent examples of the great star's signatures, including the aliases she loved to use. Garbo's A.L.S. material sells for $7,000 to $10,000 per letter, depending on content.

into the box like it was on fire, fumbling through, retrieving the envelopes, not bothering to open them. Then I sat down as quietly as possible to examine them in detail.

There was one requesting that he address her as *Hammond Brown,* others signed "GG," others signed "H" and "HB," others unsigned, and still others signed "G" and/or "Greta Garbo." They were unmistakably genuine. They were two to four pages long, all handwritten in heavy pencil, most on lined paper and each in its own envelope. My excitement was indescribable! I was holding thousands of dollars in my hands and was not yet through the balance of the material.

Following the original clue in the letter from his mother that had thanked him for sharing a letter from Garbo and that she would return any he wished to send, we retrieved the unopened correspondence. We were not disappointed. It, too, yielded some additional pieces.

Even George had the joy of making his own discovery. Sitting alone on Sunday while I was at church, half watching the TV, half rummaging through one of the boxes, he tossed away a letter but as it fluttered to the floor his half-conscious self said to him, "I think that looks familiar." He snatched it back for a closer look and, indeed, it was very familiar. It consisted of one page, partially printed and partially written, on Hampshire House stationery with the Hampshire House penciled out. He was beaming with pride when I returned.

Time and space do not allow a full disclosure of all the interesting items pulled out of our boxes of junk, nor can we explain here how all those letters, telegrams, clippings, and pictures fell into place once they were put into chronological order. Junk had suddenly become history.

Authors and autograph experts Helen and George Sanders display Helen's incredible discovery of $150,000 worth of Greta Garbo letters, uncovered at a local antique furniture auction.

We had originally searched for something of *financial* value. We were certainly successful in that, because our treasure trove is estimated to be worth somewhere in excess of $100,000. But in our search we found something else, as well. We discovered that Greta Garbo was *not* GRETA GARBO. GRETA GARBO played parts in movies. GRETA GARBO was Anna Christie and Anna Karenina and Camille and Ninotchka. Greta Garbo left GRETA GARBO at the gates of MGM and went home to be herself, sans makeup, sans pretense, sans glamour, sans GARBO!

I have spent countless hours poring over the letters we found that were written by the legend known as Greta Garbo. The letters reveal a troubled woman who disliked stardom but could never go back to the simple, normal life she'd had before she achieved her great fame.

As I look out of my bedroom window across the lake to the forest beyond and the misty mountains beyond the trees; as I watch the ducks make their duck-trails in the water and the doves and cardinals begin their spring repertoire; as I have shared in my children's happiness and heartaches; as I have had a love, lo unto forty years, that I do not justifiably deserve—I am sorry, so very sorry, for the lady we called Greta Garbo and Harriet Brown.

Sports

Heads up, autograph collectors. There's a new kid in town, and he's rapidly proving to be worth reckoning with.

For years the only sports autographs deemed of interest to "serious" collectors have been those of the baseball superstars. Well, says veteran collector and nationally known sports autograph expert, Charles "Chuck" McKean, that picture is rapidly changing. We interviewed Chuck especially for this book. Below are his insights on the new trends in sports autographs.

The Increasing Value of Football Autographs

"Baseball is still the kingpin of sports autographs, but collectors and dealers alike are starting to see the potential in other sports—and football is leading the way in price gains," McKean said.

Having collected football autographs for more than 20 years, McKeen notes that there are many similarities between the increasing popularity of gridiron heroes and that which took place for baseball players over the past five years.

"Sports as a whole were pretty much ignored by the majority of collectors for years. The only players deemed worth having by nonsports collectors were the superstars—Babe Ruth, Lou Gehrig, Jim Thorpe, John L. Sullivan, Walter Hagen, Bill Russell, and that caliber of athlete.

"Then, all of a sudden, baseball caught on, and autographs of other Hall of Famers and superstars went sky-high in value. The obvious situation of supply and demand played a key part—baseball stars who were great players and ignored by all except the hard-core sports enthusiast were not common autographs. So, players such as 'Goose' Goslin,

Every American loves *Babe Ruth*! His ink signatures are priced at $700, and his signed photographs may be priced as high as $1,600.

Authentic *Lou Gehrig* signed material is bringing very high prices among sports enthusiasts, as is material signed by Bobby Jones, Jim Thorpe, "Babe" Didrickson, Babe Ruth, Bill Tilden, Knute Rockne, Jackie Robinson, and other Hall of Fame athletes. This Gehrig piece is valued at $1,000.

'Chick' Hafey, and Ernie Lombardi were difficult signatures to find. The result was that their prices went proportionately higher than most of their counterparts.''

Scarcity

"The present situation that we see in football, and among other sports, could make the scarcity of some of those baseball autographs look relatively slight.''

What the Hillsboro, Oregon, collector believes is that because few collectors have specialized in football over the past 20 years, the signatures of all except the most standout players are in small supply.

"For whatever reason,'' McKeen said, "collectors have tended to specialize in the players from their hometown teams and not write those in other cities to try obtaining their autographs by mail.

"It might have been the stigma put on football players by some—either that because of the nature of the game they weren't nice enough to sign autographs by mail, or (in some cases) undoubtedly there was a perception that they might not even know how. The fact is that by and large football players have always been more cooperative than athletes in baseball or basketball, as far as signing autographs is concerned. And as to their intelligence, it should be noted that most players at least attended four years of college before going on to the professional ranks.''

Finding Football Addresses

One other major drawback, McKeen said, has been the lack of a major address list for football autograph collectors. "Baseball has long had the extensive lists of current and former players put together by Jack Smalling of Iowa. Home addresses for football players have been very difficult to find.

"I put out a list of some 1,000 home addresses for football players recently. That is the largest list I know of, but it doesn't even give a good start on the potential number of players autograph collectors would like to write.''

Asking *Big* Guys to Sign

Even in-person autographing has been less common for football stars than for other sports figures, McKeen believes. "Undoubtedly, part of that is because of the sheer size of many of these athletes. It isn't like going up to a baseball player, who probably is not significantly larger physically than the person doing the asking. In football, you have to

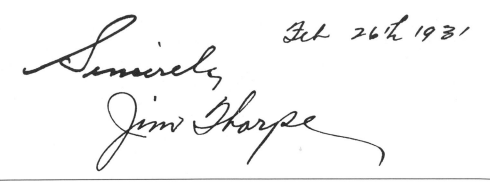

The autograph of *Jim Thorpe,* perhaps the greatest American athlete of all time, is highly desirable. Value: $400.

go face-to-face with guys who can be quite a bit bigger than you are, and that surely has intimidated many fans.''

The result, McKeen says, is that football autographs are not plentiful enough to meet a high demand situation, and that this condition is intensifying interest in the sport among autograph collectors.

Difficulty in Obtaining Autographs

''Collectors and dealers alike are aware of what happened with prices in baseball over the past few years. As they see heightened interest in football, they are starting to move into the sport and are actively seeking autographs of football greats.

''Already we're seeing football players of the past becoming aware of this. Some are charging collectors for their signature, and others are stopping signing as they receive far more requests than they have in the past.

''For the most part, this is still confined to the Hall of Fame star; they are the most easily reached and the most visible of the football stars. Again, because of the scarcity of home addresses, many other former grid greats are simply not being found yet by collectors.

''The only possible result of this is that the scarcity in football autographs will be significantly more than what we saw in baseball. Even now, when people are trying to get these autographs, they can't find the players to even ask them. This just adds yet more scarcity onto scarcity, and the end result is likely to mean a rapidly escalating price situation for football.

''That will most readily be seen first in the case of the deceased gridiron greats. Even those who died in the 1980s aren't overly common. We're talking about important

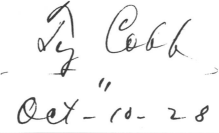

Left to right, Ted Bentley, *Ty Cobb,* Fred Haney, and George Sisler, stand behind Sanders just before a big game.

players and coaches such as George Halas and Bobby Layne. Jack Christiansen died a few years ago, Alan Ameche passed away even before he could reach the Hall of Fame, Norm Van Brocklin and Bob Waterfield died a month apart in 1983, Bill George was killed in an auto crash a couple of years before them, and the list goes on. None of those guys' autographs are available in any abundance. Some are downright scarce.

"The situation gets even tighter in the case of deceased Hall of Fame members such as Ernie Nevers, Frank Kinard, Cliff Battles, Ken Strong, or Dutch Clark. We're talking about great players who weren't actively pursued for autographs while they were alive.

"We can continue with example after example. Buddy Young, who died a few years ago, was one of the early black players. Benny Friedman, Kenny Washington of UCLA (who was the first black pro star), Buddy Parker, Mike Michalske, Ki Aldrich, Cecil Isbell, Beattie Feathers, Bobby Dodd, Bobby Grayson, Bob Reynolds, even Art Rooney, Senior—these guys are all deceased and none of them are easy autographs to find for your collection."

Items to Have Signed

Also complicating the search for football autographs, McKeen says, is that "by and large, it is more difficult to find quality items signed by former players. The situation isn't the same as in baseball, where collectors since the late 1940s were able to get Hall of Famers on first the black and white, and then on the gold plaque postcards. It's only been the past couple of years that any similar postcard was seen for football Hall of Famers, and these were basically only available from the Hall of Fame members themselves.

"There has also been a huge supply of gum cards for baseball players, available to collectors for the most part at reasonable prices. Those seeking the signatures of baseball greats on cards through the mid-1970s were blessed with a supply of cheap cards— including hundreds of reprints and original collectors' cards that made delightful vehicles for autograph-seekers.

"Those interested in football autographs were faced with a very small supply of gum cards that were not easily found in the first place. Unlike baseball, dealers have not had large stocks of old football cards for sale. At least not until recently, when interest in football skyrocketed.

"The result of all this is that there are not thousands of signed gum cards of deceased football players out there in collections. The number is probably more like hundreds for certain former players."

The Makeup of a Good Sports Collection

McKeen's own collection may well be one of the largest of signed football gum cards. "I have around 5,000 signed gum cards, with about 500 from the late 1940s through 1957.

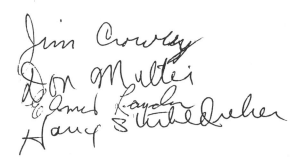

The "Four Horsemen" of Notre Dame football fame. The signatures of *Jim Crowley, Don Miller, Elmer Layden,* and *Harry Stuhldreher,* all on one sheet, are a sweet prize to behold and to frame. Value: $800.

In addition, I have approximately 1,000 signed photographs in my collection. I only keep a simple signature if that is all I can find on someone, so probably 99 percent of my collection is in the form of either signed gum cards or signed photos with a few checks also in my albums. Letters from football personalities are almost nonexistent. I only have a few."

While there are many difficulties facing those collecting football autographs, McKeen said he also feels that there are significant rewards.

Trends

"First, just because of the importance of football in our sports history, those who have made a difference in the sport should be great additions to most collections.

"Inevitably, better address lists are going to surface. I am always working on mine, and I'm sure that other collectors are doing the same. Eventually we are going to start to put together some of the various lists that collectors have and there will be a master list of 5,000 or so names. That will make the search for these men the easy part of the job.

"We're also going to see a proliferation of items to be signed. The gum cards are going to be less common than in baseball, because only in 1989 did significant numbers of cards start to be printed. However, there are many other items to get signed that make for an attractive collection—commemorative envelopes are one of my personal favorites. We are going to see more of these come out, relating both to the history of the game and to the individuals who have helped it develop to the point it has now reached.

"More and more photographs are going to be made available to collectors, to use for autographs. And almost certainly there will be collectors' sets issued, showing former players and coaches, that will be perfect for autographs. Of course, that isn't going to help in the case of scarce autographs of deceased players, but it will help the hobby grow in the future."

159

Miss Eastwood Ernst
1206 Haight Street
San Francisco, 17, Cal.

Hall of Fame quarterback *John Brodie* is one of hundreds of sports stars who have signed a George Sanders guest book in person.

The Future of Collecting Football Autographs

McKeen feels that the football autograph hobby has been at the point baseball was in the 1960s. "I think, however, that it is about to take a quick jump and won't really go through the long growing period that baseball went through. I see a rapid jump to a situation similar to those of baseball autograph collectors of the early 1980s. That is going to be frustrating for many collectors, who have begun to move into this area of autographs over the past year or two. Many of them are scrambling, hoping to pick up autographs that they missed over the years, before the prices really go up.

"I think anyone hoping for that is going to have to move very quickly, because time is running out for them. There is going to be increased competition for football autographs, and that is bound to drive prices up."

For those who are just entering the hobby, McKeen suggests that they have plenty of targets for their search. "There are great gum cards now that you can get signed, and they make a nice collection. Keep aware of relatively inexpensive quality items such as commemorative envelopes that you can get autographs on, and try to develop your own sources for photographs. After that, it is just a matter of doing your work and getting after the guys."

Cheerleaders and Other Fun

McKeen adds that a football autograph collection can also be spiced up by the addition of signatures of some of the professional teams' cheerleaders. Hmmm. Autographed photos of the Dallas Cowgirls maybe?

Says McKeen, "The take-it-serious crowd might look down on you some, but who cares! Get signed photographs of some of the individual cheerleaders for your albums. It's strictly for fun, and if you like the result, that is all that counts."

Football Is Hot!

For collectors such as McKeen, that is what football has been for many years. "It has been fun. That's it, just fun. There hasn't been any financial gain available to those of us who have collected in football, and, although it was always a mystery why the sport didn't catch on with autograph collectors, it seemed as if it would simply never happen.

"Then, all of a sudden, football has gotten hot. Growth in the hobby appears likely to be tremendous in the coming months and years. So for those who haven't been interested in football, there now is the possibility of a solid monetary investment, plus the fun and excitement of collecting in such a relatively new, untouched area of the autograph hobby.

"One thing for sure, the time to start is now! Football is about to take its rightful spot of importance in sports history as far as autograph collectors are concerned. But there's still time to get involved early enough to put together a nice collection. You might not be on the ground floor of the hobby, but the game has still just started."

Golfer Autographs: The Latest Popular Collectible

In the words of sports autograph dealer Roger E. Gilchrist, who is an above-average amateur golfer himself, ''The growing demand for good golf autographs is exceeding their supply. The burgeoning of this collecting public forges ahead in ever-increasing numbers. The availability of the better golf autographs appears to get smaller and smaller.''

When Tom Kite took a seven on a par four during the 1988 United States Open Golf Championship, the millions of amateur golfers watching in the United States and around the world had, at some time, all done exactly the same thing. When Scott Hoch missed a two-foot putt to lose the 1988 Masters Golf Tournament, these same millions all said as one, ''Even I could have sunk that putt!''

The Fastest Growing Sport in America

Golf is the fastest growing sport in America today. The United States Golf Association estimates that if a new course were opened each week between now and the year 2000, the available courses still could not keep up with the expected demand for play. Golf is played by millions. Not only watched, but *played*.

Golf is one of the few sports in which the average player identifies readily with his or her hero. As players, these millions of average golfers ''make'' a long putt, ''chip in'' from off the green, drive ''straight down the middle,'' ''get up and down'' from greens-side bunkers, make ''birdies'' and ''pars,'' and, oh yes, make ''bogies'' and ''double bogies'' as well.

The history of the game of golf plays a prominent part in the weekly televised golf events. Some of the more obscure early winners of the game are becoming more and

Golf collectibles, like this signed photograph of the legendary linksman *Bobby Jones,* have recently become some of the most expensive items in the world of sports autographs. Value: $1,200.

more familiar, joining Bobby Jones, Walter Hagen, Gene Sarazen, Sam Snead, and Ben Hogan as household names.

Many, Many Names to Collect

And what about the hundreds of other names, all very important to the history of golf? Names that until now were known only to a few aficionados, or to historians of the game. These names, found only on the Honor rolls and commemorative plaques in the dark paneled halls of the elite golf courses throughout the golfing world, now play an important role in any collection of golf autographs.

The list offered below includes many names of those who have contributed to the game of golf in one way or another—some as great players, some as architects of the world's great courses, and others as administrators or journalists. We may get frowned on for leaving out a particular name that some believe belongs in this list. No slight to anyone is intended in any way. This list is made up of the Golf Hall of Fame, United States Open winners, and other earlier "stars" who have never become household names.

The Shortage of Vintage Golf Autographs

One of the reasons for the shortage of quality golf autographs is that until the advent of the big prize money now offered by the PGA tour events, the small number of "tour" golfers traveled together and in relative obscurity. They had a charisma about them recognized by only a few of the golfing public.

When we now see movie film of those matches played before 1950, the galleries seem very, very small. Attention to the players, the principal characters, was not shown to those who deserved it until the advent of televised events. With television came recognition by millions. Some of the millions wrote to those golf "heroes." Those heroes replied, and it is those replies that are so important to the avid collector of golf autographs. So many names go unnoticed in collections because their significance remains unknown. We hope that these names mentioned below will help.

The Most Sought-After Golf Autographs

The following list contains some of the most sought-after names. See if you have any. If you do, *smile;* you are very, very lucky.

Willie Anderson	Margret Curtis	Harold Hilton
Tommy Armour	Jimmy Demaret	Ben Hogan
John Ball, Jr.	Joseph Dey, Jr.	Dorothy Campbell Howe
Jim Barnes	Leo Diegel	Jock Hutchison
Patty Berg	Ed Dudley	Robert T. Jones, Jr.
P.J. Boatwright, Jr.	Olin Dutra	O.B. Keeler
Julius Boros	Chick Evans	Tony Lema
Mike Brady	Johnny Farrell	Lawson Little
James Braid	Doug Ford	Gene Littler
Billy Burke	Vic Ghezzi	Bobby Locke
Jack Burke, Jr.	Herb Graffis	Henry Longhurst
William C. Campbell	Ralph Guldahl	C.B. MacDonald
Harry Cooper	Walter Hagen	Alistair Mackenzie
Fred Corcoran	Chick Harbert	Lloyd Mangrum
Henry Cotton	Chandler Harper	John McDermott
Bing Crosby	E.J. Harrison	Fred McLeod
Bobby Cruickshank	Corbun Haskell	Cary Middlecoff

Tom Morris, Jr.	Clifford Roberts	Jerome D. Travers
Tom Morris, Sr.	Donald Ross	Walter J Travis
Francis Ouimet	Paul Runyan	Richard S. Tufts
Henry Picard	Gene Sarazen	Harry Vardon
Horace Rawlins	Denny Shute	Glenna Collette Vare
Betsy Rawls	Horton Smith	Roberto De Vicenzo
Edward Ray	Alex Smith	Joyce Wethered
John Reid	McDonald Smith	Craig Wood
Johnny Revolta	Sam Snead	Babe Didrikson Zaharias
Grantland Rice	John H. Taylor	

This list can be endless and golf autographs are by no means limited to those of players named above. Those players who have won a PGA Tour event and many of the internationally known events all belong in a collection of golf autographs. The signature of any golf architect, any golf writer, any golf coach, or any golf official that achieved a position of note belongs in a good golf autograph collection. Because so many collectors and dealers alike do not recognize these names or understand their significance, a collection of early golf personalities is very hard to put together.

Conclusion

Autographs of baseball's deceased Hall of Fame players are the objects of a demand never before experienced. Rumors are that football may be the next sport to experience the same growth. For those of us who have been paying attention to our own passion, golf, the sport has never had enough good material to satisfy the demand. Despite its setbacks, despite the fact that so many golfers and others go unnoticed in collections and remain in piles and boxes, more and more collectors and dealers alike are taking greater notice of this part of the autographic world.

CHAPTER 12

What to Do with All That Paper

A collector of sterling silver would not leave Paul Revere pieces out in the rain to tarnish, nor where light-fingered persons could make instant profit.

Likewise, *preserving* and *safeguarding* the elements of their collections should be of concern to collectors of autographs. *Bookkeeping* and *display* are priorities in the maintenance of an autograph collection, too, and this chapter and the next are concerned with all these very important topics.

In these days of complicated taxes, bookkeeping can be extremely important, especially if you decide to sell, insure, or donate items you have collected. Proper record keeping is also a necessity in case of theft or an IRS audit.

Record Keeping

Paper can deteriorate or be defaced easily if care is not taken. In past years, collectors often would take a pencil and write the source and purchase price of a letter or other document directly on it. Many thousands of pieces now have such markings on them, or dealers' prices and comments such as "very rare."

Whatever you do, *do not attempt to erase these penciled notes*. They don't injure the paper and may be of considerable importance in establishing provenance. The handwritings of many old-time dealers and collectors are recognizable by many current dealers and collectors who have handled large numbers of manuscripts. Thus, a dealer's note written long ago can help to prove the authenticity of a piece.

Today, however, *nothing* should be written on an autograph item. Nor, for reasons we will discuss in the following chapter, should other paper come in contact with it

George Sanders's parents visited him on an RKO set where he was acting with film star *Robert Young* in 1945, long before "Father Knows Best." From left to right: George R. Sanders Sr., George, Grace R. Sanders, and Robert Young.

(unless the other paper is absolutely known to be acid-free). So records for your collection need to be kept separately from the actual collection pieces in some manner.

The simplest way to keep these records is by using index cards, which may be alphabetized by categories and easily filed. On the card for a specific autograph, the following minimum information should be recorded: author, source of the autograph, date obtained, cost, exact measurements, and any other identifying characteristics. The details that fall into the last category may be important in identifying your piece in case of loss or theft.

If you store autographs in plastic sleeves stored in a three-ring binder (an excellent storage system), a good practice on more important pieces is to type up a page with yet more information that you can place in a facing sleeve. This page can include a complete transcript of the document or letter (the preparation of which will increase your facility in deciphering handwriting). Other facts about the autograph should also be recorded, such as appearance at public exhibitions, existence of other copies, repairs, known publications, the address of the dealer from whom you bought the piece, and so on. Having this data at hand with the autograph can save you a lot of fumbling about to find it later. Including a picture of the person and biographical information also enhances the display of your collection, its value, and (most importantly) *your* enjoyment of it.

Don't Throw Anything Away

If an autograph was purchased from a dealer, save the correspondence relating to it along with the bill of sale. Reputable dealers will provide a sales slip on which they list the piece and include a description. A statement to the effect that ''all autographs are guaranteed genuine'' is usually included. If not, ask for it! There is no logical reason for a dealer to refuse to guarantee authenticity, so don't be shy in demanding it. If a dealer will not provide such a guarantee, take your money elsewhere.

When you purchase a packet of letters from the same person or a group of documents that are all related in some manner, record keeping can become a bit more complicated. In such cases, you should break the collection and the purchase price down and assign a pro rata value to each piece. This holds true also for unrelated items which you may purchase for one lump sum. Record keeping may seem onerous at the time, but doing it at the time of purchase is *much* easier than trying to reconstruct it years later (especially if an IRS auditor is breathing hotly down your neck).

George Sanders on a Warner Bros. movie set with comedian Alan King, actress Cara Williams, and actress Ann Blyth in 1957.

Hitting the Old Audit Trail

"Audit trail" is an accounting term which means that a way exists in a bookkeeping system to show where funds and assets came from and where they went. In today's information age, there are two ways to keep track of the things you own and the value they have: on paper, and by use of a personal computer. Over 20 million Americans now own or have the use of a personal computer, and this method is fast becoming the best way to handle personal finances.

Computers, by the way, have become relatively inexpensive these days. You can get a complete IBM-compatible setup now, including a printer, for well under a thousand dollars. Because of this relative affordability, more and more people are enjoying the benefits and the power of personal computing.

Chapter 14 of this book discusses in detail the process of managing your collectibles using a computer, but let's talk here about computerized accounting for a moment. And, please, don't throw your hands in the air and say this is too complicated. We'll keep it simple, and you can apply these same techniques in paper-based accounting—it just takes a lot longer.

There is a program available now for IBM and IBM-compatible computers ("clones") which fills the job very nicely and quite inexpensively (one of the authors does all his personal accounting using it). The program, called Quicken, is sold in most computer stores or can be purchased via mail order (see any computer magazine) for around $50 to $60. It was chosen the product of the year in 1988 by several computer magazines. You should be able to save the purchase price of the program in taxes the first year, simply because you will have more exact records.

What such a program does is organize our finances, forcing us to be accurate, complete, and up to date (which is what most of us need help with). As your autograph hobby grows, you may find that having such organization garners you considerable money as you sell off duplicates or even sell off various collections as your fields of interest change (as mentioned earlier in this book, autographs are a good investment if you buy wisely and selectively).

A computerized accounting program like Quicken can automatically do all the necessary bookkeeping drudgery (in 14 steps in the case of Quicken) to pay your bills, and it can hand you printed checks already addressed for mailing. It can also give you instant insight into your finances with detailed reports on cash flow, profit and loss statements, balance sheets, and more.

Quicken will ease the April 15 blues by giving you detailed reports on taxable income and (important!) each tax deduction. It also interfaces with various popular tax preparation software programs. The IRS, believe it or not, is finally getting modern and will now accept tax returns in certain personal computer formats. You can even let your computer call in your taxes on the phone line (consult with an accountant on the proper procedures).

Other advantages of computerizing your accounting procedures is that you can track all your assets and liabilities, have instant net worth statements, and monitor loan balances and capital investments.

The Importance of Proper Accounting

Regardless of how you do your accounting—whether on a spiffy new computer or on dime-store tablets with a gnawed stub of a pencil—we urge you to take the time and do it right. Keeping track of your hobby adds to its enjoyment. Proper accounting also has the nice side benefit of ordering your life and taking some of the hassle out of it. It all adds up to more fun and, equally as important, more time to engage in the engrossing hobby of autograph collecting.

Care and Preservation

Regardless of how precise your record keeping may be, computerized or not, the actual autograph itself must be kept in the very best condition possible. Proper preservation will ensure that your collection will retain and probably increase its value over the years.

There are several good books that discuss the subject of autograph care and preservation. Two of the better sources are *Autographs: A Collector's Guide,* by Jerry E. Patterson (Crown, 1973), and *Collecting Historical Documents,* by Todd Axelrod (TFH Publications, 1984).

Red Tape

Older documents suffer from being folded. Before the invention of the file cabinet, papers were usually tied up in bundles with string or ribbon for storage. The English government often used red tape instead of string to bundle documents, thus spawning the term "red tape" as it applies to bureaucracy.

It is not uncommon to find bundles still tied and folded in this manner. Should you acquire one of these, immediately unfold each piece and place it between two pieces of acid-free paper and onto a flat surface for gradual unwrinkling. A weight, such as a book, may be placed on top, as long as it does not come in contact with the document. All paper clips, pins, ribbons, and so on should be removed. Wax seals, if intact (which is rare), should be left in place.

Explorer *William Clark* (of Lewis and Clark fame) signed this voluminous document in 1784. Value: $1,500.

Acid

Many pieces of paper carry the seeds of their own destruction deep within: *acid!* Dealers and librarians can tell horror stories of autograph collections preserved in folders or framed in which the paper degenerated or was left with stains and other unsightly damage.

Acid occurs naturally in wood. One look at an old ''pulp'' magazine from the 1930s—pages yellowed, tattered, and crumbling—can immediately show you how this internal destructive process affects paper. For that matter, last year's newspaper can show you the same thing. Older paper, from the nineteenth century and earlier, usually had a higher rag content than modern paper does and thus had a lower acid content.

As a rule of thumb, the higher the pulp content of the paper, the greater the acid content. Newsprint, the cheapest kind of paper, has the most pulp content, but even newspapers, pulp magazines, and old comic books (which also have a high pulp content) can be preserved. In fact, a good bookstore carrying collectible comic books can be of great benefit to the autograph collector. The better ones sell such preservation materials as acetate bags and deacidification sashes. These latter items actually remove acid from paper, dramatically increasing the paper's life. For valuable pieces on cheap paper, these sashes can be a very worthwhile investment.

The mistake some collectors make is to put a related newspaper clipping in the same folder with an autograph piece. Even though the autograph might be on good paper, the acid in the newsprint can quickly stain and even ruin the autograph document. So put autograph items in an acetate folder, and protect them from coming in contact with other paper!

Acetate folders are also available at most stationer's stores, as well as at stores specializing in stamp or photography supplies. Even if these folders are designed for holding comic books, stamps, or photographs, they are just fine for autographs, too. Always ask for *acid-free* material.

Learning from Stamp Collectors

We autograph collectors can learn a lot about preservation from stamp collectors. Stamps are usually more delicate and more likely to fade than autograph documents. Pages sold for philatelists are quite useful for storing and preserving autographs.

Buying acetate folders already punched for a three-ring binder makes your storage problems a lot easier. You can have a notebook for each category of your collection: Civil War, U.S. presidents, sports, vintage movie stars, etc.

If you have a manuscript of several pages, remove all paper clips and staples because these will rust and discolor the paper if they remain attached. The general rule here is to let nothing but protective acetate come in contact with an autograph piece. Engravings, newspaper clippings, and even photographs (which are sometimes still coated with chemicals) should be stored in a separate sleeve or folder.

Circular

Treasury Department
January 20th 1790

Sir

Notices friendly to the Interests of the Office of the Customs, as well as to the advancement of the public service, induce me to desire that I may be as soon as possible furnished with a statement of the amount of the emoluments which have accrued to them respectively under the existing regulations up to the first of January. As this letter will only be addressed to the Collector of each district it will be proper that a communication should be made to the Naval Officer and Surveyor.

I shall take it for granted that the information I may receive on this head will be such as I may place absolute reliance upon.

I am, Sir,

Your Obed. Serv.

A Hamilton

Alexander Hamilton is one of several great American statesmen who were never president but whose letters and documents are popular as framed memorabilia. Value: $600 to $1,000.

Beware Humidity

Acid is not the only enemy of paper; humidity can be quite destructive, too. Excessive humidity, such as that which often is present in a basement or garage, can lead to mold on papers stored in such areas. Some geographic areas, such as the southeastern United States, can be especially hazardous to books, stamps, and autographs that are stored in an uncontrolled environment. If you have a humidity problem, the purchase of a dehumidifier for the room your autographs are stored in is a very wise investment.

You may also place small packets of silica gel (the stuff that is packed with new cameras and radios) inside binders, etc. These packets soak up water vapor from the air, but they must be replaced after a period of time. The relative humidity should never be more than 70 percent in a room where autographs are stored, and about 50 percent is ideal. Cold is no problem.

Shedding Light on the Subject Is Not Always Good

Another enemy of autographs is light, especially ultraviolet-laden direct sunlight, which is particularly destructive. If you display an autograph in a frame, you can use ultraviolet shields to protect them, both from the sun and from artificial light sources.

Dust can also be harmful. The shelves where you keep your collection should be kept clean. The same is true for filing cabinets, if those are used. Dust can carry particles of various chemicals that deteriorate paper.

In general, there is nothing wrong with taking an autograph out of its storage place for an occasional airing, just as stamp collectors air stamps. In fact, air circulating around paper is usually beneficial. No autograph should be sealed up too tightly.

Framing, Matting, and Displaying Pieces

As we've just seen, light is an enemy of autographs. The simple fact of life is that light causes ink on paper to fade. Ultraviolet shields, nonreflective glass, and the like can inhibit this fading action, but nothing except total darkness forever will completely guard against light's harm. Therefore, a really valuable autograph, such as a George Washington letter, should not be framed and displayed. A better choice for framing might be an autograph of a favorite actor, actress, baseball player, or whatever your interest runs to in current celebrities.

If you do frame and hang a piece (and a framed autograph can look quite awesome in your living room), *never* place it where direct sunlight has a chance of hitting. Reflected daylight is also dangerous, causing fading, as is fluorescent lighting. The plastic ultraviolet shields already mentioned will help protect against the worst of light damage.

Framing or even matting (placing the autograph between two pieces of cardboard-like material with a hole cut in the top one to frame the item) takes a modicum of skill, tools, and materials. If you collect and/or sell a lot of autographs, this craft is well worth learning and will quickly pay for itself. Professional framers charge professional prices.

For the occasional piece, most people go to a framing shop. When you entrust an autograph document or letter or signed photograph to a framer, some precautions are in order. First, you must insist that the matting board used should be "museum board," meaning it is acid-free. The thickness of board chosen should be one which will keep the autograph from touching the glass of the frame and also allow for some air circulation.

Explain vigorously to the framer that clear tape, masking tape, or any other kind of tape should *never* be used, nor should the autograph be pasted down in any manner, not even to prevent wrinkling or buckling. The framer, also, must not be allowed to cut or trim the piece in any way. Engravings or photographs framed with the autograph must not be allowed to touch it either.

Computerizing Your Collection

Collecting is the largest hobby in the United States and Canada. A lot of us collect in several categories—autographs, of course, included.

That awesome technological spinoff of the space program, the personal computer, is the answer to many a collector's prayer. No matter what kind of collecting you participate in, keeping track of your collection increasingly becomes more and more of a formidable task as you acquire more and more pieces. This is particularly true for small items, because several hundred units may make up the collection—or several thousand.

Comic books, baseball cards, magazines, stamps, butterflies, dishes, postcards, coins, beer coasters, glasses, political campaign buttons, *autographs*—these and other types of collectibles present cataloging problems that the personal computer is ideally suited to solve. Organization via a computer can make collecting so much more fun because it enables you to know what you have to trade, what you need to buy, what duplicates you have, the numerical totals of the various classifications of your collection, and so on.

The nice thing about being a collector and living in a fast-expanding high-tech age is that the personal computer becomes more powerful and less expensive on almost a daily basis. For just a few hundred dollars now, any one can own a small desktop computer that a few decades ago would have cost several hundred thousand dollars and filled an entire room with its circuitry.

Now, however, such personal computers as the many brands of IBM-compatible "clones" and others of use to collectors are readily available at prices most people can afford. The information age is upon us in a wondrous flurry of high-tech gadgets, and practical computerization is no longer the province of large corporations or big government. Average people can have them in their own homes—and they're fun!

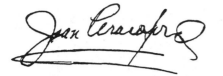

Academy Award–winning actress *Joan Crawford* shares an anecdote with Sanders at the 1954 world premiere of Alfred Hitchcock's "Rear Window."

Database Management

Computers excel at four basic jobs: accounting, word processing, repetitive calculations, and database management. While the collector may find peripheral uses for the first three capabilities, it's database management that's the godsend for cataloging book upon book of autographs, boxes upon boxes of comics, thousands of political campaign buttons, and articles from any type of collection under the sun.

A database is simply any group of facts about interrelated items—things that fall into some common classification. Let's say, for example, items in an autograph collection (since that's what this book is about). You may have several notebooks with transparent plastic sleeves, each book containing scores of autographs. Such facts as the total number of autographs, the number of baseball signatures, the number of Hollywood entertainer pieces, the related values, and all other important facts about the autographs in your collection are data available from the database, once you have set it up (a process described later under the heading "Sorting").

The concept of management, of course, we're all familiar with—the ordering of events or facts to yield desired results. Database management is quite simply managing the facts associated with your collection. A database manager program allows you to enter and retrieve these facts quickly and easily. It will alphabetize and generate reports for you, giving a total of your holdings and what each individual piece is worth, either for a single category—for example, artists' autographs or eighteenth-century autographs or autographs acquired in a certain year—or for the collection in its entirety.

The computer does what would literally take you hours in a minute or two at the most. This same concept can be applied to any type of collection, from matchbook covers to bus tokens, from rocks to military memorabilia. At any time you can pull out any of the hundreds of facts about your collection according to any set of criteria you may devise. This adds a new dimension to the fun of collecting. At any time you can know exactly what is in your collection, how it breaks down, what you have too much of, what you may want to add, what you may want to trade or sell off. All this and more from that little box on your desk—your personal computer doing database management.

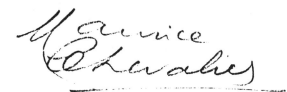

French singing star *Maurice Chevalier* was congratulated by Sanders during the 1959 Academy Award ceremonies in Hollywood.

Order from Chaos

Any collector over a moderate period of time can easily accumulate thousands of small items. Even if your autograph collection is small now, we guarantee you that it won't be for long. That's the marvelous insidiousness of collecting—once we get hooked on accumulating something, we go for the gusto, so to speak. The four or five comic books quickly proliferate into hundreds; the small box of political campaign buttons suddenly seems to become several large boxes full to the brim; the Fiestaware collection spreads from the dining room like some vast, multicolored tidal wave to take over the whole house; your beautiful stamps suddenly number in the thousands; autographs seem to multiply on their own; and so on and so on. We lose sight of individual items, forced into mere approximation of our collections rather than being aware of each and every piece. Just finding and categorizing pieces become daunting tasks that we feel are best put off for a nonspecified and usually hypothetical rainy day.

The personal computer (running the appropriate programs) changes all this. It is indeed the answer to the collector's prayer, adding fun to our hobbies by bringing order out of chaos, exactitude from sloppiness. Any competent piece of collectible-oriented software will achieve this end by performing several types of jobs for you.

Sorting

Sorting is one of the single largest and most necessary tasks required to organize any collection. Sorting is simply making a list of what's in a collection based on any of several criteria.

For instance, you might want to list the thousands of items making up your collectible holdings alphabetically by the name of the signer of the autograph, or numerically by the arbitrary inventory number you've assigned at time of acquisition, or by quantity of duplicate pieces in either ascending or descending order (most common or rarest). Additionally you might want to sort by size, by condition, or by several other different classifications. You might even desire a number of different lists at once (and most likely will upon seeing how easy a computer can do this for you). Lists that before were

Sir Wallace E. Rowling was the prime minister of New Zealand when this photo was taken with Sanders, acting Director General of Radio New Zealand in Wellington. Rowling is now New Zealand's ambassador to the United States.

impractical because of simply being too time-consuming and too much work can now be produced and updated every day, if you so wish.

Collectibles-oriented programs (or more general standard database managers) handle this sorting in two major steps. The first is the initial start-up, which is the only part about computerized collecting that is even vaguely hard. The bad news is that you have to key into the computer an initial entry for every single piece in your collection; in so doing you must include all the data pertaining to each and every item.

This sounds like, and is, a considerable amount of work, but the payoff in efficient, enjoyable management of your collection from that time forth more than pays you back for the time spent punching the keyboard of your computer. Besides, your collection will only get larger. So doing this chore *now* is really easier than putting if off to that illusory rainy day we've already mentioned. (And don't forget to keep your records up to date by keying in an entry for each new piece you acquire.)

Which brings us to a quick aside. Any collection you work at for years grows considerably in value. A few hundred dollars for a computer to manage it effectively becomes a quite reasonable expense after all. Such an investment can increase the value of your collectible holdings through more efficient trading and selling of duplicates. You can even eventually become a dealer and make a partial or full-time living from your hobby.

Software for Autograph Collectors

The term *software* simply means a computer program (as opposed to *hardware,* which is the actual computer equipment). The authors of this book are currently developing several computer programs of interest to autograph collectors which will be available soon.

The first is a facsimile "generator." This program lets you type in a name and see an authentic depiction of that person's autograph on the screen. As we saw in the chapter on forgeries, it is very important to be able to compare pieces to examples that are known to be authentic.

Our second program is an extensive one designed to manage an autograph collection. It is based on the very powerful program we wrote to do *The Price Guide to Autographs.* (For that venture the program was already handling over 50,000 prices, so developing it into a program that can keep track of most collections is moderately simple.) If you would like more information on software for autograph collectors, contact us via Autograph House, P.O. Box 658, Enka, NC 28728.

Emceeing his Emmy Award–winning television documentary series "Success Story," George Sanders interviews Academy Award–winning director *Frank Capra*.

Conclusions

There are other ways to keep records for an autograph collection, too. Ledger books and loose-leaf notebooks are two tried and true methods. However, the advent of the computer age is proving to be a boon to many collectors. Autograph collecting, being in essence the management of large amounts of data, lends itself well to record keeping via a personal computer.

Again, the fact that a good IBM-compatible system, including printer and monitor, can now be had for under a thousand dollars makes this option more and more attractive. Whether it is a hobby or a business, autograph collection should be and can be fun. A computer eliminates much of the bookkeeping drudgery.

A full explanation of the myriad of computerization benefits for collectors is beyond the scope of this book, but the basic two programs needed are a database manager and a word-processing program.

Going to an autograph show? A database enables you (and your computer) to print out a list of what you have so you can avoid buying duplications. Found a listing in a dealer's catalog for a football player you may or may not have? Don't thumb through your albums or card index looking when all you have to do is key the player's name into the computer and have all the pertinent information pop up on the screen.

The other program you need, word processing, speeds up correspondence and allows neatly formatted and automatically spell-checked descriptions to be included in autograph albums. As already detailed, such extras enhance the value of your collection and can increase your enjoyment of it.

A computer is just a tool, like a hammer. Properly used, a computer can enhance your hobby, and make it even more profitable, in terms of both money and pleasure.

CHAPTER 15

The Ultimate Autograph Collection

As you gain knowledge and additional experience in this exciting hobby, your ambitions will grow, your tastes will probably vary, and your dreams will begin to include some of the autograph world's most treasured manuscripts, letters, and photographs.

On the following pages (as well as scattered throughout the rest of the book) we have included a few examples of some of the aforementioned gems that are available on today's market. At your leisure you can study letters, documents, signatures, and signed photographs of some of the greatest people who have ever lived and thus experience the true magic of autographs.

The prices indicated on some examples represent certain market trends whenever a letter has a special and historically worthwhile content or has that "rarity factor" that has been discussed at length elsewhere in this book. Someday, if you choose, items like these will adorn the walls of your home or apartment, fill your leather-bound loose-leaf books, or be donated by you to your favorite college or private institution.

Now, turn the pages and dream the *possible* dream....

IRVING BERLIN

September 27th, 1967

Mr. Leon Gutterman
Wisdom
9107 Wilshire Boulevard
Beverly Hills, California

Dear Mr. Gutterman:

Many thanks for sending me the Wisdom Book
devoted to David Sarnoff.

I'm certainly looking forward to reading this
tribute to one of our great Americans.

Again my thanks and with best wishes, I am

Sincerely,

Irving Berlin

I
B
:
h
s

Composer *Irving Berlin* was only 79 years old when he dictated this thank-you letter in 1967. He died in 1989, soon after celebrating his 101st birthday. Value: $850.

This is the last page of a lengthy message from composer *Georges Bizet*, who wrote the opera *Carmen*. Value: $2,000.

Evolutionist and clergyman *Charles Darwin* wrote this letter in 1875. Value: $4,000.

A handwritten letter from composer *Johannes Brahms* (1833–1897). Value: $2,000.

The final page of a lengthy letter from *Empress Catherine the Great* (Catherine II) (1729–1796) to her general and lover, Count Gregory Orlov. Value: $2,800.

French landscape painter *Jean Baptiste Camille Corot* (1796–1875) wrote this letter in the final year of his life. Value: $1,200.

BRANCH HOUSES, KANSAS CITY & ST. LOUIS, M?

INCORPORATED 1868.   BY STATE AUTHORITY.

DEERE & COMPANY

Moline, Ill. May 22 1878

John Deere Moline Plow Works,
ESTABLISHED 1847.

In reply to yours of

The A. S. S. U
Gents
I received notice of my appointment
by your Board of Managers, as one of
the Vice Presidents of the Board.
I thank you for the honor & will do all
in my power for the glorious cause
Respty, Yours
John Deere

The handwritten letters of this inventor-industrialist are seldom seen. Agricultural products have made the *John Deere* name known throughout the world. Value: $1,000.

München, den 9. Oktober 1889.

Hochverehrter Herr Geheimrath!
Für die freundliche Zusendung Ihrer
Uebersetzung von Dante bitte ich Sie hier-
durch meinen verbindlichsten Dank em-
pfangen zu wollen. Sollte ich einmal nach
Wiesbaden kommen, werde ich gewiss nicht
versäumen denselben mündlich zu wie-
derholen.
Mit unseren herzlichsten Grüssen habe
ich die Ehre, mich zu zeichnen
Ihr ganz ergebener
Henrik Ibsen.

Autographs of Norwegian dramatist and poet *Henrik Ibsen* (1828–1906) remain in demand by collectors. Letters such as this one are rare. Value: $950.

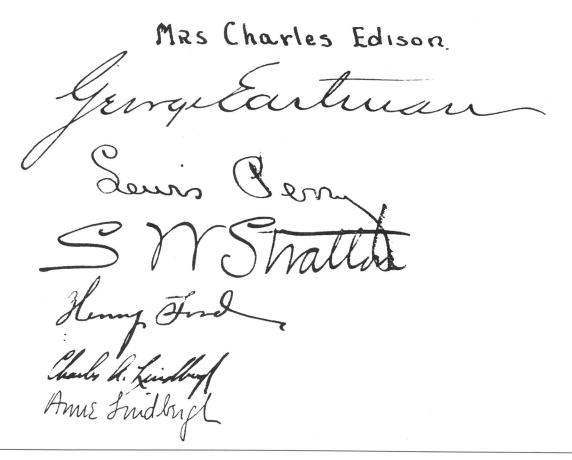

Mrs. Charles Edison printed her name and then assembled an incredible array of signatures of famous people on a single album leaf: *George Eastman* (Eastman-Kodak); industrialists *Lewis Perry* and *S. W. Stratton* (Briggs-Stratton); auto-maker *Henry Ford;* and *Charles and Anne Lindbergh.* Value: $1,500.

The signature of the first black heavyweight boxing champion, *Jack Johnson,* commands top prices. Johnson's career inspired the Broadway hit "The Great White Hope" which renewed interest in the superb boxer. Value: $300.

Dear Mrs Thegpen :

After two futile attempts
to be clever I give up and merely
sign myself

March 3d, 1923

Regretfully
F Scott Fitgerald

F. Scott Fitzgerald, author of *The Great Gatsby*, wrote this brief note to a fan. Value: $1,000.

Dear friend
I was thankful
for your note of
reminder. You
will all be
most welcome.
Please expect
a friend at Ahmeda
bad station to
escort you to the
Ashram.
yours sincerly,
29
39
MKGandhi

Mahatma Gandhi—statesman, father of a nation, India's greatest twentieth-century figure, and the beloved inspiration of millions—penned many letters, but there are not enough to satisfy collectors' demands. Value: $1,500.

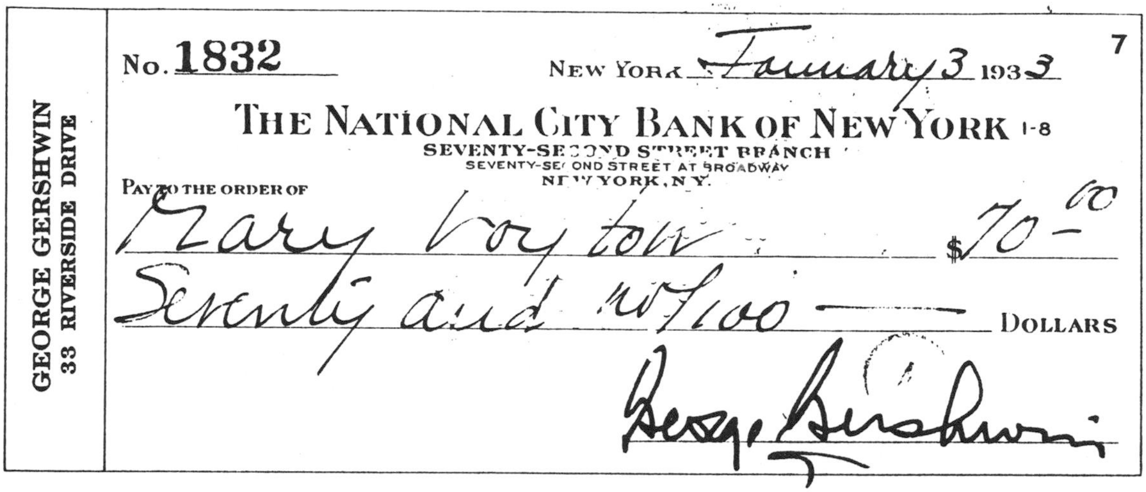

No. **1832**   NEW YORK *January 3* 193*3*   7

THE NATIONAL CITY BANK OF NEW YORK 1-8
SEVENTY-SECOND STREET BRANCH
SEVENTY-SECOND STREET AT BROADWAY
NEW YORK, N.Y.

GEORGE GERSHWIN
33 RIVERSIDE DRIVE

PAY TO THE ORDER OF *Mary Voyton* $70 —

Seventy and no/100 ——— DOLLARS

George Gershwin

George Gershwin, the Brooklyn boy who became one of America's greatest composers, left behind some of the loveliest music ever written but not too much material for autograph collectors. Value: $1,000.

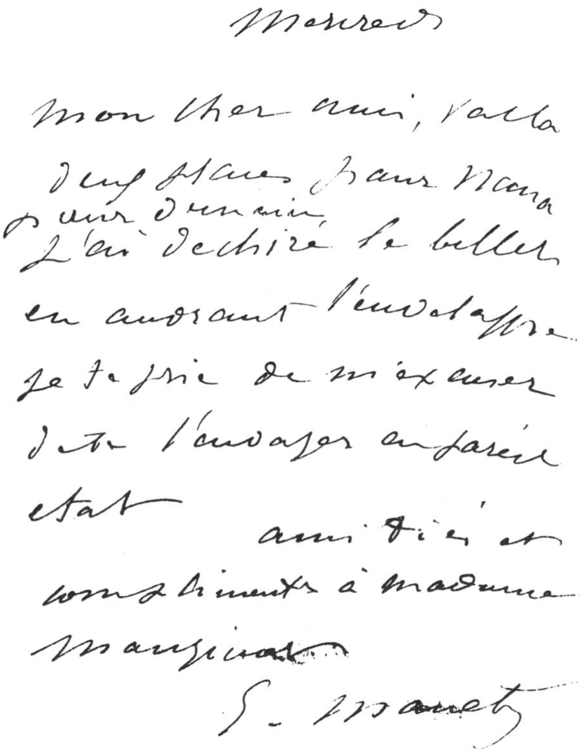

[handwritten letter in French]

Letters by Parisian artist *Edouard Manet* are scarce because of his early death at age 51; missives such as this are quite rare. Value: $1,200.

The painter who built the first steamboat, *Robert Fulton,* was not the most prolific writer of letters. His material is highly prized. Value: $1,500.

Dear Sir

I will endeavour to do myself the pleasure of Waiting upon you this Evening

Yours Sincerely

Robt Fulton

New York
March 15. 1861.

Sir, I herewith cheerfully comply with your request of the 13. instant

Respectfully
Yr Obedient

Saml. F. B. Morse.

O. K. Brooks, Esq
Cleveland
Ohio.

The autograph of painter *Samuel F. B. Morse,* who built the first telegraph instrument, is much sought after by collectors who specialize in either the arts or science. Value: $1,000.

Scarboro Me

*June 9th 189_*

Dear Ernest—

I leave here on Monday next—, I may go from Boston direct— to Albany, some time next week. & may go to N.Y. but I shall bring up at the Clubhouse by the last of the week hoping to see you & Arthur,

Yours very truly

Winslow Homer

Give my regards to your Father

This A.L.S. of artist *Winslow Homer* would be a welcome addition to the walls of many American homes. Such a piece is attractive to collectors because it can be framed with a print of the artist's work to make an impressive display. Value: $1,000.

played golf there - outside of
atlantic city and a wonderful
course - Quite a few people
are there over Easter and it's
usually fun -

I didn't get the part
in the Melvyn Douglas show - I
really don't think I'm too
young for the part - if any-
thing he is too old - and
just too conceited to admit it -
Robert Joseph — who co-produced
"The Father" is going to do
"King Lear" next fall - Harold
Clurman is going to direct -
I'd give my eye-teeth to do
Cordelia —

I signed a lease today
for my apartment in Manhattan
House - I think I told you
about it — a view of downtown
and the river - with balcony -
I'll draw the plan on the
other side — '"

Before she became Her Serene Highness the Princesse de Monaco, actress *Grace Kelly* was a highly impetuous romantic. This is one of her "love" letters to a married man she met while she was working in New York City. Such gossipy letters have interesting content and thus bring high prices from dealers. Value: $1,750.

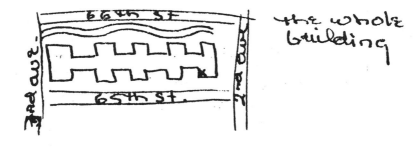

the whole building

my apartment –

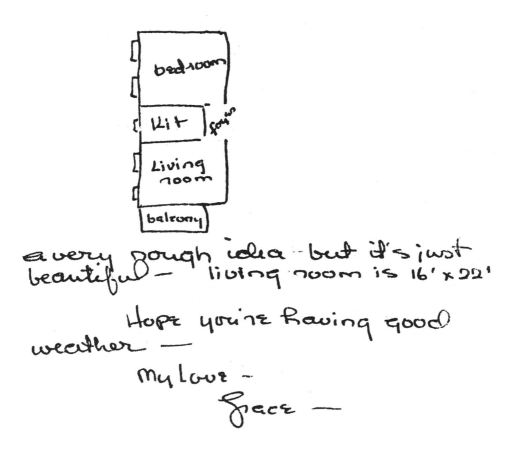

a very rough idea – but it's just beautiful – living room is 16' x 22'

Hope you're having good weather –

My Love –

Grace –

This Indenture made this nineteenth day of January in the year of our Lord eighteen hundred and twenty four between John W. Baker of George Town District of Columbia of the one part and Francis Scott Key of the same place of the other part Witnesseth that whereas Walter Smith hath this day by the order and direction of the said F S Key conveyed to the said John W. Baker, by deed bearing the same date with these presents, a certain piece or portion of land lying in Washington County in the said District, as by the said Deed will appear, and whereas the said John W. Baker stands indebted to the said F S Key in the full and just sum of three thousand five hundred dollars, a part of the purchase money of said land (the sum of one thousand dollars the residue of the purchase money for said land being paid or secured to be paid to the said F S Key) and hath passed to the said F S Key his several nine promissory notes bearing date the ninth day of January in this present year for the payment of the said sum of thirty five hundred dollars and the accruing interest thereon, in nine equal

Famous attorney *Francis Scott Key* gave us the national anthem—and this indenture, which bears his signature 16 times in its entire text. Look for the "F.S. Key" notations.

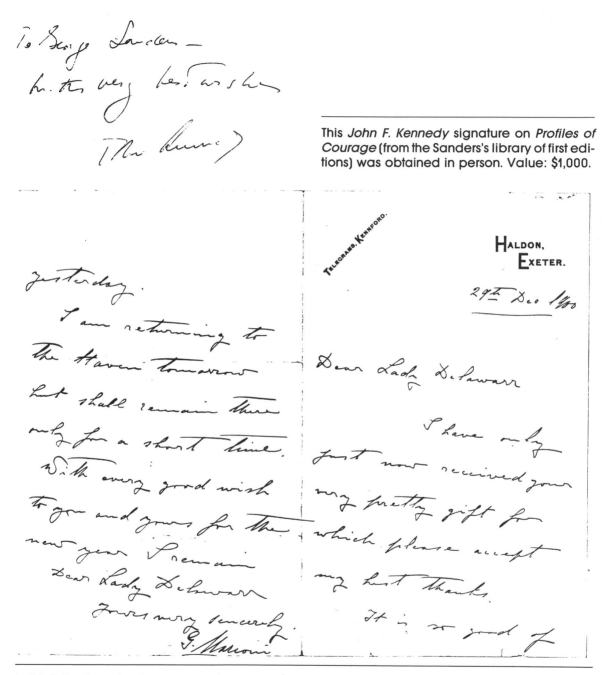

To George Sanders —
for the very best wishes
[The Kennedy]

This *John F. Kennedy* signature on *Profiles of Courage* (from the Sanders's library of first editions) was obtained in person. Value: $1,000.

HALDON,
EXETER.

TELEGRAMS, KENNFORD.

29th Dec 1900

yesterday.
I am returning to
the Haven tomorrow
but shall remain there
only for a short time.
With every good wish
to you and yours for the
new year I remain
Dear Lady Delawarr
Yours very sincerely.
G. Marconi

Dear Lady Delawarr

I have only
just now received your
very pretty gift for
which please accept
my best thanks.
It is so good of

In this letter, inventor *Guglielmo Marconi* discusses his work with the wireless. Such special content warrants the piece's $1,000 price tag.

Another example of an artist's A.L.S. that cries out to be framed with a copy of the artist's work. This *Henri Matisse* would sell for approximately $1,300.

Pierre Auguste Renoir's letters, which show the tiny handwriting of an artistic giant, are not common, even in France. This letter, which has excellent content, would cost about $1,600.

MARGARET MITCHELL

Atlanta 5, Georgia

June 2, 1948

Dear Mr. Remacle:

      Your charming surprise package reached me safely and has given me so much pleasure. Thank you for it and the kind thoughts that went with it. The chocolate candy has a delicious flavor---I never tasted any like it.

      I have thought of you many times since our conversation so many months ago and wondered if you found the people for whom you were searching. For a long time I have wished to explain why I did not personally assist you to a greater extent than I did. My husband has been ill for two years and he is now recovering, but during the period when you were in Atlanta he was not well and I seldom left our house. I have thought of you with remorse, that I did not go to your assistance, for you were a stranger and a guest in our town, and I am sorry I could not do more for you.

      Again many thanks.

Cordially,

Margaret Mitchell Marsh

Margaret Mitchell Marsh

(Mrs. John R. Marsh)

Margaret Mitchell, author of the highly popular *Gone with the Wind,* died at an early age. She was featured on a U.S. postage stamp, and her letters are prized possessions. Value: $1,500.

Many collectors are now specializing in signed "White House cards." When such a card contains an A.L.S., as does this *William McKinley* piece, the price reflects its rarity. Value: $825.

Playwright *George Bernard Shaw*'s letters are interesting, peppery, and frequently egotistical. This A.L.S. provides an excellent example of his caustic wit. Value: $1,000.

The signature of *Napoleon Bonaparte* has always been a popular item, but never more than now. The galleries that frame such material cannot keep "the Little Emperor" in stock. Because of its excellent content, this document is valued at $1,500.

8/7 1817.

Very Respectfully
I am sir
Y. Obd. servt.
O. H. Perry

I. B. McKean Esq...

Your letter of the 14 inst ...
me, and in reply thereto I have to inform
you that there is no prospect of my
taking an active command for some
time to come - I therefore highly approve
son & nephew obtaining orders

A.L.S. material by *Commodore Oliver Perry* is not common. Value: $750.

Anything autographed by *Robert Louis Stevenson* is treasured by collectors. Value: $750.

Author and master dreamer *Jules Verne* remains a popular figure with autograph collectors. Although this A.L.S. is brief, it would still be priced in the $1,000 range.

Inventor *Eli Whitney* wrote windy letters with little humor, but their rarity brings an A.L.S. like this one to the $1,500 price level.

Count Ferdinand von Zeppelin gave us the dirigible airship and a new word; however, while the word *zeppelin* is fairly common, the count's letters are not. With excellent content, a piece such as this is worth $1,000.

will you then come to the studio (8. Fitzroy Street)
on Tuesday afternoon at 5. o'clock ?

        Kindly send me a line to
say if this will suit your plans
for that day - or will you
propose another ? -

               Very sincerely
               Jms Neill Whistler

1. Orwell Terrace
   Dovercourt

     I hope you have good news of your
         brother

Sep. 6. 1901

The art world's stormy petrel, *James McNeil Whistler*, would probably roll over in his grave if he discovered that his handwritten letters were commanding figures as high as $1,500. He sold some of his original art for less than that during his lifetime.

Resource List: Autograph Dealers, Galleries, and Publications

We have selected the following dealers, publications, and galleries because the proprietors and staff have the patience and expertise to educate novice collectors who will become future customers. For a more broad-based, exhaustive listing of dealers, publications, and galleries, see *The Price Guide to Autographs,* by the authors.

Antique Week
Tom Hoepf, Editor
P.O. Box 90
Knightstown, IN 46148

Autograph Collector's Magazine
Joe Kraus, Editor
P.O. Box 55328
Stockton, CA 95205-8828
(209) 473-0570

Autograph House
George & Helen Sanders
P.O. Box 658
Enka, NC 28728
(704) 667-9835

Robert F. Bachelder
Eileen Keiter, Mgr.
1 West Butler Ave.
Ambler, PA 19002
(215) 643-1430

Catherine Barnes
P.O. Box 30117
Philadelphia, PA 19103
(215) 854-0175

Walter R. Benjamin Autographs
Mary Benjamin
Christopher C. Jaeckel
255 Scribner Hollow Rd.
Hunter, NY 12442
(518) 263-4133

Carolina Senior Citizen
David George, Editor
66 Flint Street
Asheville, NC 28801
(704) 251-5881

Christie's
502 Park Avenue
New York, NY 10022
(718) 784-1480

Collector's News
Linda Kruger, Editor
Box 156
Grundy Center, IA 50638

Herman Darvick Autograph Auctions
Herman Darvick
P.O. Box 467
Rockville Centre, NY 11571-0467
(516) 766-0093

Sophie Dupre
Clive Farahar
14 The Green, Cane
Wilts SN11 8DQ, ENGLAND
(0249) 821121

Gary Hendershott
P.O. Box 22520
Little Rock, AK 72221
(501) 224-7555

Librairie de l'Echiquier
Frederic Castaing
13, Rue Chapon
75003 Paris, FRANCE
274-69-09

Lion Heart Autographs, Inc.
David H. Lowenherz
12 West 37th St. (Suite 1212)
New York, NY 10018
(212) 695-1310

James Lowe Autographs, Ltd.
30 East 60th St. (Suite 907)
New York, NY 10022
(212) 759-0775

Maggs Brothers, Ltd.
Miss Hinda Rose
50, Berkeley Square
London W1X 6EL, ENGLAND
(01)-493-7160

The MidAtlantic Antiques Magazine
Kay Crumpston, Editor
P.O. Box 908
Henderson, N.C. 27536

National Pastime
Harvey Brandwein
Stephen Hisler
93 Iselin Drive
New Rochelle, NY 10804
(914) 576-1755
(718) 224-1795

Neal's
192 Mansfield Rd.
Nottingham, NG1 3HV ENGLAND
0602-624141

Paper and Advertising Collector
Doris Ann Johnson, Editor
Box 500
Mount Joy, PA 17552

Cordelia & Tom Platt
1598 River Rd.
Belle Mead, NJ 08502
(201) 359-7959

Profiles in History
Joseph Maddalena
9440 Santa Monica Blvd. (#704)
Beverly Hills, CA 90210
(800) 942-8856

R & R Enterprises
Bob Eaton
1 Overlook Drive
Amherst, NH 03031
(603) 672-6611

The Kenneth W. Rendell Gallery, Inc.
Kenneth Rendell
The Place des Antiquaires
125 East 57th Street
New York, NY 10022
(212) 935-6767

Riba Auctions, Inc.
Brian Riba
P.O. Box 53, Main Street
South Glastonbury, CT 06073
(203) 633-3076

Paul C. Richards
Gerard A. J. Stodolski, Associate
High Acres
Templeton, MA 01468
(800) 637-7711

Joseph Rubinfine
505 South Flagler Drive, St. 1301
West Palm Beach, FL 33401
(407) 659-7077

Safka & Bareis Autographs
Bill Safka & Arbe Bareis
P.O. Box 886
Forest Hills, NY 11375
(718) 897-7275

Searle's Autographs
Pat & Charles Searle
P.O. Box 849
Woodbine, GA 31569
(912) 576-5094

Swann Galleries, Inc.
George S. Lowry
104 East 25th Street
New York, NY 10010
(212) 254-4710

Tollett and Harman
Bob Tollett and Donn Harman
175 West 76th Street
New York, NY 10023
(212) 877-1566

U.A.C.C. Auctions
P.O. Box 6181
Washington, DC 20044-6181

Wallace-Homestead Book Company
Chilton Way
Radnor, PA 19089

John Wilson (Autographs) Ltd.
50 Acre End St.
Eynsham, Oxford OX8 1PD
ENGLAND
(0865) 880883

Yesteryear
Michael Jacobi, Editor
Box 2
Princeton, WI 54968

Annotated Bibliography

Benjamin, Mary A. *Autographs: A Key to Collecting,* privately printed, 1963.

No history of autograph collecting would be complete without mentioning that premiere autograph dealership, Walter R. Benjamin Autographs. Over the years, the company has had only two managers—Walter R. Benjamin and his daughter, Mary A. Benjamin. Ms. Benjamin's book is a collection of the knowledge garnered by her father and herself over many years. Contact Mary Benjamin at Walter R. Benjamin Autographs, 255 Scribner Hollow Rd., Hunter, NY 12442, (518) 263-4133 for information concerning this fine book and its availability.

Berkley, Edmund Jr. *Autographs and Manuscripts,* Scribner's.

This useful and scholarly reference work presents a good overview of signed material.

Carr, Paul. *The Universal Autograph Collectors Club's Study of Machine Signed Signatures,* U.A.C.C., 1989.

Edited by Al Wittnebert, this book acquaints the reader with machine-signed signatures. It establishes that anyone who is anyone in Washington, D.C., has an automatic signature machine, and it helps you determine what is real and what is machine-generated. Contact U.A.C.C. (Universal Autograph Collectors Club), P.O. Box 6181, Washington D.C. 20044-6181.

Darvick, Herman N. *Collecting Autographs,* Julian Messner, 1981.

Herman Darvick, who is based in New York City, has become the leading auctioneer of autograph material in the United States. Darvick is a longtime autograph dealer, and his 1981 book, while aimed at young readers, still contains much valuable information and is a welcome addition to the reference shelves of any serious collector. Mr. Darvick may be contacted at Herman Darvick Autograph Auctions, P.O. Box 467, Rockville Centre, NY 11571-0467, (516) 766-0093.

Hamilton, Charles. *American Autographs,* University of Oklahoma Press, 1983.

It would be impossible to say too much about Charles Hamilton and his stature in the world of autograph collecting. He has long been the "dean" of autograph writers. His decades of experience as a dealer and auctioneer of autograph material combine with his professional writing talents to create interesting and fact-filled books.

Hamilton, Charles. *Signatures of America,* Harper & Row, 1977.

Hayes, Jim. *War Between the States, Autographs and Biographical Sketches,* Palmetto Publishing, 1989.

This book is primarily aimed at giving the autograph collector and Civil War buff a single-volume reference in which to look up almost anyone of importance from that era. Contact Jim Hayes, Antiquarian at P.O. Box 12557, James Island, SC 29412, (803) 795-0732.

Koschal, Stephen. *Collecting Books and Pamphlets Signed by the Presidents of the United States,* Patriotic Publishers, 1982.

Among autograph collectors, it is well known that the signatures of United States presidents are highly prized and very desirable. Nothing moves faster from any dealer's stock than documents, letters, and photos autographed by the presidents of the United States. The author details the collecting of these premium pieces, with special emphasis on books signed by presidents.

Marans, M. Wesley. *Sincerely Yours,* Little, Brown and Company, Boston, 1983.

This collection of autographed photographs gives the reader a sense of intimacy with an extraordinary assemblage of overachievers since the invention of photography in 1839. Over 400 signed portraits, many by major photographers, have been selected from what is surely the world's most important collection of autographed photographs.

Patterson, Jerry E. *Autographs: A Collectors Guide,* Crown, 1973.

An older book that is still often found in libraries. This volume is packed with excellent information.

Rawlins, Ray. *The Stein and Day Book of World Autographs,* Stein and Day, 1978.

This book contains facsimile autographs of about 1,600 famous and infamous individuals. They come from all walks of life, from about 70 nations, and from the eighth century to the present. This book is of great use to the serious collector, the archivist, and the librarian, and it will certainly entertain the layman.

Reese, Michael. *Autographs of the Confederacy,* Cohasco Publishing, 1981.

An excellent and specialized look at Confederate Civil War notables only. Recommended for the serious collector of Civil War material.

Sanders, Sanders, and Roberts. *The Price Guide to Autographs,* Wallace-Homestead, 1988.

The Price Guide to Autographs is *the* price guide in the autograph field. It lists current prices in every category for tens of thousands of collectible autographs, letters, notes, signed photographs, and documents.

With the use of sophisticated computerization, the authors have compiled prices realized by auctions in the United States and abroad. They have added to those figures the current prices gleaned from over a hundred U.S. and foreign dealers, placing heavy emphasis on material offered by full-time autograph dealers.

Features of the price guide include special articles for the beginner, contributed by some of the best-known names in the autograph world; information on how to preserve autograph material; over 1,500 facsimiles of genuine signatures; and over 50,000 prices.

Signed copies of *The Price Guide to Autographs* or this volume, *The Collector's Guide to Autographs,* may be ordered from the authors by writing to Autograph House, P.O. Box 658, Enka, NC 28728.

Searle, Charles and Pat. *From the Inkwells of Hollywood,* 3 volumes, Woodbine Press, 1989.

Charles and Pat Searle, well-known experts and dealers in entertainment autographs, and co-owners of a San Francisco autograph gallery, have put together a definitive series of facsimile books. These books are an invaluable reference in checking the validity of signatures of both current and vintage entertainers. With the wide usage of secretarial signing in Hollywood from the very first, references like the Searle books are a necessity. Contact Searle's Autographs, P.O. Box 849, Woodbine, GA 31659, (912) 576-5094.

Sullivan, George. *Making Money in Autographs,* Coward, McCann, & Geoghegan, Inc., 1977.

This book describes how to profit by selling letters and documents of the world's notables.

Taylor, John M. *From the White House Inkwell,* Charles E. Tuttle, 1968 (just reissued).

The author provides information on the autographic scarcity of each of the presidents. Included are such illustrated items as autographed photographs, inscribed books, handwritten poems, telegrams, and vouchers, as well as franks, commissions, ship's papers, land grants, and warrants. The illustrations alone are worth the price of this book.

Vrzalik, Larry F. and Michael Minor. *From the President's Pen, An Illustrated Guide to Presidential Autographs,* State House Press, 1990.

The authors have provided analyses of the autographs and writings of each U.S. president from George Washington through George Bush. They entertainingly tell us which president's signature is the scarcest, the most ornate, the most valuable, the friendliest, and the most illegible.

Wittnebert, Al. *Signatures of the Stars,* U.A.C.C., 1988.

No collector of Hollywood material can consider his or her reference bookshelf complete without this guide to Tinsel Town signatures. Contact U.A.C.C., P.O. Box 6181, Washington, D.C. 20044-6181.

Index

About the Authors

George Sanders has been collecting autographs for 50 years. As a radio newsman, TV anchor for Exxon news, newspaper columnist, and actor (appearing in over 20 motion pictures and on television), Sanders naturally began to collect the signatures of the hundreds of celebrities with whom he came in contact. He has also been a writer, college professor, and a business executive in the U.S. and abroad.

Helen Sanders is a celebrity in her own right. A graduate of Pasadena Playhouse and a starlet in the late forties in Hollywood, an actress who worked with Tennessee Williams, a professional photographer whose work has appeared in hundreds of publications, a radio and TV performer for over 30 years, and the author of numerous magazine articles, Helen, too, has had many opportunities to mingle with other celebrities.

George and Helen Sanders own Autograph House, which has one of the nation's most extensive privately held autograph collections, encompassing over 20,000 historical documents, letters, signatures, and manuscripts. Having bought and sold autographs with a total worth of over a million dollars, the Sanders are well versed in authentication, evaluation, and other services and topics of concern to autograph collectors. Autograph House will help collectors find pieces for their collections and make fair market offers on significant pieces that collectors have for sale. (Interested collectors should contact Autograph House by mail at P.O. Box 658, Enka, N.C. 28728, or by telephone, during normal business hours, at 704-667-9835.)

Ralph Roberts has sold 18 books and over 2,500 articles and short stories to publications in numerous countries. His work includes literally hundreds of articles on antiques, autographs, and other collectibles.